Oh, MIND
RELAX PLEASE

Roots of Yoga
Wings of Management

SWAMI
SUKHABODHANANDA

Author of all time best seller
MANASE RELAX PLEASE

Published by Prasanna Trust
300/18, 6th Main, 14th Cross, Vyalikaval Bangalore 560 003, India

Year of publication : January 2002

First Edition	– No. of copies :	5,000
Second Edition	– No. of copies :	3,000
Third Edition	– No. of copies :	3,000
Fourth Edition	– No. of copies :	5,000
Fifth Edition	– No. of copies :	5,000
Sixth Edition	– No. of copies :	5,000
Seventh Edition	– No. of copies :	5,000
Eighth Edition	– No. of copies :	5,000

Cover Design : Suresh UT

Book Layout : Govardhan Kini K

Printed at
SUDHINDRA
Malleswaram, Bangalore 560 003

ISBN 81-901496-0-1

Price : Rs. 225/-

Acknowledgement:
Viswanatha Subash, Gurunandan Mulky, B.S. Prasad & Preetpal Dahele.

ii

REFLECTION

**If you serve the universe;
the universe will serve you.**

Reflect on this incident: -

Fleming, a poor Scottish farmer, heard a cry for help. A boy mired to his waist in black muck was struggling to free himself. Fleming saved the boy.

Next day, an elegantly dressed nobleman came to Fleming & said, 'You have saved my son. I want to reward you for your act'.

'No, I cannot accept any reward for my act. It was my duty,' replied Fleming.

'Is that your son?' the nobleman asked pointing to the lad standing next. Fleming nodded in affirmation.

The nobleman offered to educate Fleming's son as a goodwill gesture. 'Your son will make you proud' was his assurance.

Years passed. Fleming's son went on to become Sir Alexander Fleming, who discovered Penicillin. Years later, the nobleman's son was stricken with deadly pneumonia. What saved him? 'Penicillin vaccine.'

The name of the nobleman was Lord Randolph Churchill. His son was Sir Winston Churchill.

Someone said, what goes around comes around.

There are two types of actions; outer & inner. What determines the quality of one's life is the inner action – thoughts and emotions. Be alert to every moment in your thoughts & emotions and learn to relax.

As you read this book, you will be sensitive to your thoughts and emotions. Observe the gaps between the thoughts and emotions. It is in these gaps your life will start flowering and relaxing.

Gift this book to your friends and relatives; let the law of grace emerge and lead you to inner peace.

With blessings,

SWAMI SUKHABODHANANDA

FROM THE AUTHOR

I have always told myself if I cannot be happy here and now, I will never be happy anywhere. This book is an offering of my happiness.

The superficial way of reading this book is through intellectual understanding. The deeper way is by feeling the insights of the narration. The deepest way is where these insights and parables light up your mind in your hours of darkness and guide you like a friend.

Hence my invitation is to read this book not just once, but many times over like a daily prayer....... for prayer is not changing the Lord but changing you.

By ingesting the essence of this book, you will realise what lies before you and behind you are nothing in comparison to what lies within you. Enlightenment is looking for spectacles that are sitting right on your nose. This book is about awakening you.... like a wake up call.

To do what you like and like what you do is indeed a divine work. Work is an opportunity to find oneself. This book helps you in finding yourself in all walks of life... intimate, family, work, social, and spiritual zones. In the process, you will be grateful to the weeds of your mind. They ultimately help your practice of being relaxed.

Being relaxed is wise. Begin with being wise and you will be relaxed. Being relaxed is a wise and an easy way to live life.

Life, thus lived will bring forth the peace of a rose garden and light of the luminous Sun as a part of your being.

Let your growth bring the best seasons of your life. This is my humble prayer for you.

I specially thank P. R. Madhav for editing this book. My special thanks to Mrs. Devki Jaipuria for all her support. My salutation to my loving mother who is a living Goddess. My deepest gratitude to all my Gurus for whom I have no words to express. I offer this book to all my students who are like little lamps shining in the night, which the great Sun cannot do. This is my dream and I am sure you will join me in making it as your destination.

With blessings,

SWAMI SUKHABODHANANDA

FOREWORD

'Losing is victory postponed'

'World will forgive failures, but will not forgive people who have not utilised the opportunities'.

This book contains many more such thought provoking maxims. Swamiji presents complex Vedantic truths in a simple manner like a sugarcoated pill. The name Oh, Mind Relax Please! itself creates curiosity among the readers.

This book blends the truths expounded by Allah, Krishna, Christ, Buddha, Mahaveera ..... and gives many insights to the readers.

This book provides solace and counsel to people who run away from the day-to-day problems of life. Swamiji's teaching guides one not to be upset with the problem; instead take problem as a challenge and solve it energetically.

This book is unique in its presentation where narrations are real life instances in the form of parables which touches the readers' heart. Besides, this book can be read from any chapter, but still it will stimulate the reader – like a pealed banana, which can be eaten from any side, thus enjoying its sweetness.

Every insight presented in this book teaches us how valuable our life is. If one digests and uses the rich wisdom, one will attain peace in life.

CHIRANJEEVI
The Mega Star

Our heartfelt thanks to all enlightened masters & modern thinkers for their inspirational guidance.

CONTENTS

Tips for reading this book

This book is designed to provide an all-round understanding of life. Modern education has led us to more literacy and less understanding. To snatch even 15 minutes time from the routine, is a luxury that many can ill-afford these days. But there is a need for us to nourish our souls with understanding. This is the dilemma that many of us are placed in.

- One can start reading this book from any chapter; each chapter is complete by itself.

- Let this book be your constant companion. If you are free for 5 minutes, read one chapter.

- If you are free for 3 minutes, turn to the icon of the Laughing Buddha. Every story and example communicates some thing deep for you to reflect on.

- If you have only 15 seconds, read the gist of each chapter.... in the form of Yoga of Wisdom and Yoga of Action. Discover how relevant they are to your busy life.

- In case you are not able to spare even 15 seconds, just glance through any page on Contemplation. It will lead you to inner peace.

- If you are in doubt as to which chapter will be of interest... read the contents page for a variety of questions. Identify your question and read the respective chapter.

- Whenever you have a question or doubt, just open any page with reverence and read on, especially the section of Contemplation or Reflections. You will find an answer in a mysterious way.

- This book has to be read in small doses and many times over to impart a conscious shock to one's mechanical life. Make this your family book. Let your family members read one chapter either in the morning or while retiring for the day. Read out at least one story every day to your children and bathe them in wisdom.

Weed out anything that is superfluous in your life. Remember to carry this book with you always. All you need is a commitment to spare as little as 5 minutes of your time. Magically, you will enjoy being secure and insecure as well. This understanding in small and simple doses will make you relax in this tense and busy world.

The purpose of living is the very life itself.

SUCH IS THE WAY

As I have noticed, people the world over raise the same question when in great distress. Their language may vary, but they mean the same – 'Why does God burden me alone with so much strife?'

Whenever someone asks me this question, I relate a brief tale narrated by the Buddhists.

There was a small village. A young boy went to a nearby river to play at the edge of the water. As he was playing, he heard a cry for help . . . 'Oh, please save me, please save me!'

Looking around, he found a crocodile caught in a net; unable to escape, the crocodile cried out pitifully to the boy. The boy, however, was reluctant to save the crocodile, feeling that if he saved it, the crocodile was sure to eat him up. But the crocodile pleaded with him, tears streaming down its face, and said, 'Honestly, I promise you that I won't devour you. Please save me!'

The boy, convinced of its sincerity, began to cut the net that imprisoned the crocodile. No sooner was its head free from the net than the crocodile grabbed the boy's leg in its jaws.

1

Now it was the boy's turn to cry out in tears, 'Hey, you dirty croc! Is this fair?' The crocodile responded philosophically, 'What to do? Such is the way of the world! Such is life!' and continued to devour the boy.

The boy was not worried about dying. What he could not accept was the total ingratitude of the crocodile and its philosophy.

While his leg was slowly sliding into the jaws of the crocodile, the boy looked at the birds on a nearby tree and asked:

'Is the crocodile uttering the truth? Is this the way of the world - full of injustice? Is this how life goes where words are not honoured?

And the birds replied, 'We take such care to build safe nests on the tops of the trees for protecting our eggs. Yet, snakes come and swallow them. We concur with the crocodile that what it is saying is totally true. There is injustice in the world.'

Then the boy saw a donkey that was grazing on the banks of the lake and repeated his question.

'While I was young, my master loaded soiled linen on my back and extracted maximum amount of work from me. Now that I am old and feeble, he has abandoned me saying that he cannot feed me. So there is nothing wrong with what the crocodile is saying. Such is the way of the world. There is injustice and unfairness in the world and such is life!' said the donkey.

The boy, still unable to accept these explanations finally noticed a rabbit and repeated his question. The rabbit said, 'No, no! I cannot accept what the crocodile is saying. It is utter nonsense!'

Hearing this, the crocodile became angry and wanted to argue with the rabbit, even while holding the boy's leg in its strong jaws. The rabbit protested, saying that as the crocodile's mouth was choked with the boy's leg, it was not able to decipher what the crocodile was trying to say. The crocodile laughed heartily at this and said, 'I am not a fool! If I let go, the boy would run away!'

'Now, you are really stupid!' said the rabbit. 'Have you forgotten how strong your tail is? Even if he runs, you can smash him with just one mighty lash of your tail!'

The crocodile fell for this and releasing the boy, continued its argument. The rabbit screamed to the boy, 'Run! Run! Don't just stand there!' and the boy took to his heels.

Only when it tried to raise its tail, did the crocodile realise that it was still entangled in the net. As the boy ran away, it glared at the rabbit in a terrible rage.

The rabbit smiled sweetly and quipped, 'Now do you understand? Such is the way of the world! Such is life!'

In a short while, the young boy returned with the villagers and they killed the crocodile. A dog that came along spotted the rabbit and started chasing it. The boy screamed at the dog 'Hey, listen! This rabbit saved my life. Do not attack him.' But alas, before the boy could intervene, the dog had chased and killed the rabbit in a jiffy!

The young boy unable to bear the tragedy, cried and said to himself, 'What the crocodile said was true. Such is the way of the world. Such is life!'

Buddhism speaks of the same great truth that the ancient sages of Hinduism revealed – we cannot fully understand the many aspects that cover our lives.

Unfairness is a part and parcel of life. Such is the way of life. Can we teach ourselves not to be victims of unfairness and confront it with the understanding that the mysteries of life cannot be fully understood?

Such acceptance of unfairness would give us the maturity to live life wisely.

Reflections

Yoga of Wisdom
Watch – Mystery of Life is beyond our Comprehension. We are mysteriously complete.

Yoga of Action
There is far more peace in acceptance than in resistance

Contemplation

Unfairness is a part and parcel of life.

A crocodile remains a crocodile even if dressed in silk.

He that kills shall be killed. He that cheats shall be cheated.

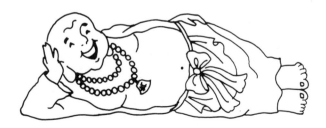

SECERETS OF PARENTING

The beautiful atmosphere of the Ashram encompasses the serenity around it. It is very pleasant to be in the Ashram. One mother experiences unpleasantness all around her. The serene atmosphere of the Ashram makes no difference to her. She shares her concerns for the upbringing of her children in this world. How was she to keep them away from drugs, alcohol and glamour?

She cries with fear and pain 'Swamiji, my life is miserable whenever I think of my children in this wicked world. What should be my approach to the bringing up of my children?'

Often I question the very genesis of such an enquiry. When we operate out of fear, we transmit the energy of fear to our children; in a subtle way, of course. If we were to operate out of trust, we would transmit trust to our children.

We have to realise that our actions are born from our thoughts. Our thoughts are the products of our values, and values come from our own belief system. If we believe life is miserable, we attract misery; if we believe life is beautiful, we attract happiness. This is called the Law of Attraction.

We get what we focus on; so focus that good things would happen to our children. This is one of the strong variables, which would impact our children.

But the mother asks lovingly 'Why do children detest advice?'

The question is, are they really against advice or the way we administer it? Every parent should be sensitive to this aspect.

Reflect on this story:

A money-minded son after having his lunch, wrote a note to his mother that she owed him $25 and he gave a detailed account - $ 5 for cleaning the house, $5 for washing the dishes, $15 for mowing the lawn. The mother was shocked on reading the note. She however decided to educate her son.

In turn she kept a note on the dinning table, which read 'Oh! Son, you owe me nothing.' My account runs like this:

$ 0 for cooking your food

$ 0 for washing your clothes

$ 0 for ironing your dress

$ 0 for cleaning your bathroom

$ 0 for taking you to the Doctor

$ 0 for the present on your birthday

$ 0 for taking you to the school and bringing you back

Finally, dear son, you owe me nothing; because I love you.

The son read this note and was deeply touched.

Children are not against advice; but they are very sensitive to the way it is administered. The heart of education is the education of the heart.

'How can I learn to advise in this manner?' asks the mother.

Reflect on this:

> Have you observed birds building nests? They build in such a way that when it rains, not a drop of water falls in the nest. How did the mother bird learn the art of such an engineering feat? It is said that when the mother bird is pregnant, intuitively this knowledge arises. Love for the offspring brings out this latent wisdom to build the nest.
>
> Let your love guide you and not fear.
> Love will show you the way.

The mother nods in affirmation that love is the supreme power. She further asks, 'How to deal with children's boredom despite the variety in entertainment through media?'

Reflect on this story:

A boy complained to his grandmother, 'No one likes me at school and life is bitter. My teachers reprimand me, friends are better than me in sports, some friends are better than me in studies and I feel bitter about life.'

'Shall I make a cake for you?', asked the grandmother.

'Good, I badly need to sweeten my life', said the boy.

After some time, she gave him flour. 'This is not cake, it is so bitter', screamed the boy. Then she gave him little baking powder.

Again the boy screamed, 'This is not cake, it is so bitter'

Then she gave him an egg.

'This is not cake, it is not tasty', screamed the boy.

Then the grandmother lovingly told the boy, 'Individually each one of them is not tasty but when put together; it becomes a cake.'

'In the same way', she said, 'individually your experiences are bitter; but join them together with commitment and transformation. Add the sugar of your being and make it a cake. Life is like cooking, you should just make it.'

Reflections

Yoga of Wisdom
Power of Love is God.
Love for Power is Ego.

Yoga of Action
Love recognises opportunities and
does not wait for its introduction.

Contemplation

Children are not against advice.

Life is like cooking, you should just make it.

It is an unhealthy bird that fouls its own nest.

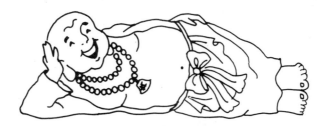

THE ANT AND ITS PHILOSOPHY

*T*his is a typical narration from what I recently encountered.

A person who met me said, 'I was born in Bombay, and am now settled in New York. I leave home at 7.30 a.m. for work and am back only at 8.30 p.m. I have to achieve my organisational goals and at the same time give quality time to my wife and family. I am tense and I don't know how to go about organising my life... and I find that my life is imbalanced.'

I said, 'The fact of life is, you are busy and have chosen to be in a busy city. It is your choice. Now add one more dimension to your choice . . . inspite of this fact I will learn to be relaxed, balanced and make my relationship work beautifully. Life is like painting and not arithmetic. The painter chooses to create his own world through his art.'

The person asked, 'What should I do, in spite of my busy schedule, to give quality time to my wife & family, still be relaxed and proactively go about reaching my organisational goals?'

I said, 'You should observe an ant and learn to organise your life. Ants overcome life-threatening obstacles in this vast world.'

'An ant?' he questioned.

If you observe an ant, you can learn a lot.

- Whatever obstacles you place in front of an ant, it is so flexible that either it goes around it, under it or above it. Flexibility is a great quality in an ant.

- An ant never quits and it is focused on its goal. It has the attitude of 'Winners never quit; Quitters never win.'

- When it is summer, it plans for winter – Tremendous planning ability.

- When it is winter, it waits patiently for summer – Patience.

- At any given point of time, it does all that is possible; it is holistic in whatever it does, however small it is, never invalidates its strengths – Commitment to do its best.

- It operates in a TEAM – Team is Together Empowering to Achieve More.

- Ants have the humility to follow the Leader- Humility is Strength; not Weakness.

- United they build an ant-hill - an engineering feat – where even cooling effect is taken care of, inside an ant-hill – Team and Team Intelligence.

- Ants, while moving in a chain, have perfect co-ordination to send feedback to the ants following them about the path they are treading on. This communication chain has perfect networking – Communication Chain.

'Can you organise and balance your life like an ant?', was my advise. I elaborated further saying we can ask these questions by comparing an ant's qualities:

- **Flexibility:** Are you flexible in giving quality time to your family? Can you appreciate your wife in a way that is life nourishing? Can you see flexibility is the mother of creativity?

- **Planning:** In summer, when everything is going well, are you planning for winter? Or are you lost in your joy?

- **Patience:** In winter, during difficult days, are you wise enough to develop the quality of patience and have an understanding of the seasonal changes?

- **Enjoy each moment**: Can you consider every incident as joyous and totally rejoice in the present rather than desiring that one or some of your joyous moments be permanent?

- **Commitment**: Are you giving your best to the present moment? Are you allowing yourself to better your best and make it a habit to be fully involved in everything?

- **TEAM**: Can you drop the 'I' in you and operate from 'WE' and make your family a team?

- **Humility**: Can you be humble to follow the rules of life rather than treat rules as binding forces? Can discipline become a harnessing force?

- **Networking ability**: Can you meticulously network with people in accomplishing higher tasks?

By following this philosophy, let the results speak.

Have you created a successful ant-hill?

Oh, Mind Relax Please! and allow relaxation to create balance and peace thus making your struggles sacred.

Reflections

Yoga of Wisdom
Life is like Painting and not Arithmetic.
Create your world of Joy.

Yoga of Action
Follow the Wisdom of the Ants.

Contemplation

What the human mind can conceive, believe and dare, it can surely accomplish.

Our struggles have a cosmic purpose.

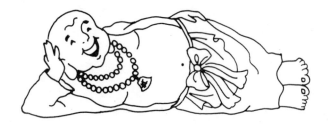

RELATIONSHIP –
A SACRED STRUGGLE

A lady with strained eyes, beaten up feelings and a forced smile, asked me, 'I feel life is miserable, my marriage did not work out, hence I am divorced; my son constantly falls sick, financially I am in a bad shape, I am struggling. Do all these have some purpose or is God playing with me and having HIS fun? I become impatient and restless in my office work. How shall I handle my impatience and my misery? I feel terribly tensed. Is there a way out?'

With deep compassion, I said, 'If your marriage has failed, can you not treat failure as a learning experience? Failure is a fertilizer for success. Failure is God's or nature's purpose to teach us something profound.'

'How can I do that?' asked the lady.

I said, 'Many times relationships do not work because men and women are not sensitive to each other's comfort and discomfort zones. This unawareness leads one to tread into the other's discomfort zone.

Once this happens, one is unhappy and feels the other responsible for it. Then each one is busy maintaining a

19

score of one's hurt and settling accounts with each other. To be aware of each other's sensitive zones helps in understanding each other very well.

'There is so much of struggle in my life, why?', cried the lady.

I asked, 'Are you a sportswoman?'

'Yes', she said in a soft voice.

I asked her, 'In sports don't we struggle to reach the top?'

'Yes', the lady answered.

Struggle is a part and parcel of life. Make your struggles sacred, give them eyes to see, ears to hear, and heart to feel, legs to walk. Then you would have implanted sacredness in your struggle, which in turn will lead you up the ladder of success.

'This would take time', she said.

One should learn to wait with understanding and commitment.

Reflect on this story:

 A man went to a shop, picked up a beautiful cup and said 'My god! this cup is so beautiful.'

Suddenly the cup started talking to the man. "Oh, man, I am beautiful right now, but what was the state of my being before the pot-maker made me so beautiful?'

I was sheer mud when the potter pulled me out from mother earth. I felt wreathed in tremendous pain while being separated from mother earth. But the potter said, 'Just wait.' Then he churned me. I felt giddy when I was churned, and asked him 'Why are you so cruel?' The potter said 'Just wait.' Then he put me into an oven and heated me up. I felt completely burnt. There was tremendous pain and I asked him again 'Why are you so cruel?.' He said 'Just wait.' After that he poured hot paint on me and I felt the fumes and irritation. I again asked him ' Why are you so cruel?' He again said 'Just wait.' He put me into an oven and heated me to make me strong, I felt life was so painful hence pleaded with the potter to leave me free. He said 'Just wait.' And finally he took me to a mirror and said 'Now look at yourself.' Lo, what a change! I found myself so beautiful."

We have to wait; our struggles have a cosmic purpose. When our agenda is not fulfilled, it gives us pain. But the universe has its own plans. We have to wait and make our struggles sacred.

Oh, Mind Relax Please!

Reflections

Yoga of Wisdom
Surrender to the Cosmic plan;
do not be a victim to your agenda.

Yoga of Action
Make your struggles sacred. Greatness lies not in
being strong but in the right use of sacred strength.

INTELLECT IS AN ANT LIFE IS AN ELEPHANT

Some time back I had been to Baroda to give a discourse on the Bhagavad Gita. There, a lady sought to meet me alone. As soon as we met, she began to weep uncontrollably. Since I felt that she would feel relieved if she poured out her heart, I encouraged her to talk. She said, 'I don't think any one else in this world has suffered the way as I have. I am going through such misery' and continued to narrate her story.

'Even when as I was a little girl, my father used to molest me to satisfy his lust. Though I was utterly devastated inside, I did not know how to stop him. As I grew into womanhood, my father continued his incestuous behaviour. I continued to suffer sexual abuse from him. Every day that dawned, brought total darkness to me. Later I got married. My husband was very loving. But my sufferings did not stop. My father did not change his habit and continued to fulfil his sexual need through me. As I could not tolerate this any longer, I revealed everything to my husband in the hope that he would free me from this hell. But as a result of this, my husband also deserted me. Why? Why has this happened to me?' she asked and wept bitterly.

I could have replied to her question with the help of the Hindu scriptures...I could have explained to her that 'This is the result of your deeds of the previous birth - Your karma! Now you have to suffer like this.' Or, I could have explained it away on the basis of psychology saying, 'Perhaps your mother may not have satisfied your father sufficiently. Or may be your father is suffering from some kind of mental abnormality and would not have sought medical aid for the malady.'

If any one could answer the question posed by that lady as to why she had to suffer such a fate, then we could find a reason as to why persons such as Hitler and Mussolini were born in this world. We could also find a way to prevent such villainous persons from being born again!

What can you learn from this example?

If we can compare our intellect to an ant, then life in this world is like an elephant.

 An Ant screamed, 'Oh! Elephant, please come out. I have to talk to you urgently.'

The Elephant came out of its herd and asked, 'Hey! Little fellow, why are you screaming? What are you up to?'

The ant said, 'I want to ensure that you are not wearing my swimming trunks.'

How could the swimming trunks of an ant fit the elephant?

Isn't it ridiculous? Our intellect is like an Ant. It cannot comprehend the mysteries of the world..... life is like an Elephant.'

But, just because we give explanations like the one above, it does not mean we should tolerate everything; silently bear insults and harsh treatments from other people.

We should learn to be assertive, not aggressive. Assertive people would never give up their rights. They would not allow others to encroach onto what is their right. We should face all the odds that we come across and fight them. But, whatever the end result of all these struggles, we should have the mental maturity to accept it as 'Such is the way of the world and such is life!'

Understand that life is not cruel, but full of mysteries. Mystery is to be felt rather than to be solved. In experiencing the mystery of life, an intuitive ability emerges like a mother bird building a nest for its offspring. How did it learn? It is the power of love.

I asked the lady if we were to have this attitude where is the question, 'Why me?' This question would not arise. Pain and suffering would not touch us.

Perhaps this prayer may help you.

> 'Oh God! Give me the strength to change what I ought to change,
>
> Give me the courage to accept what I cannot change and
>
> Give me the serenity to know the difference.'

Reflections

Yoga of Wisdom
Watch - Many things are beyond our comprehension. Life is not a problem, but a mystery

Yoga of Action
Hug each moment of your life and nourish your connection to the universe

A CAT TETHERED TO A PILLAR!

What is prayer?

Here, I am entering into the aspects of God and Spirituality. We need to think deeply on the subject. The essence of prayer is the ability to totally understand ourselves. A prayer is not just words, descriptions or sounds. It is mainly the sacred understanding of ourselves with devotion.

Prayer is not getting entangled in mere rituals without understanding their meanings.

Here, I have to relate something. Recently I had been to a house where I encountered a very different kind of morning prayer or 'Suprabatham.' 'Kousalyaa suprajaarama... hey, Alamelu! The milk is overflowing, please, turn off the gas! Rama poorvaa... sandhyaa... Gopu! Why is that fan just on for nothing? Pravarthathe... uthishta...'

I am not narrating a joke. It is just not prayer. Lighting the lamp, tying up a string of mango leaves, performing arti, etc., and other spiritual practices are performed as mere rituals these days. Many of us perform them mechanically without understanding their meaning. This is a fact found among people of all communities and races. For example, tolling a bell in a temple is to awaken oneself to the God within, not to awaken the God outside. How many of us do this with understanding?

There was a Guru who had mastered the scriptures such as Vedas and Upanishads. One day, when he was teaching Vedas to his disciples, a cat was moving around. This, however, did not disturb the Guru, but was a distraction to some of his disciples. So, the Guru instructed his disciples to get hold of the cat and tether it to a pillar to prevent distraction. As this nuisance continued to recur on the following days, the cat was regularly tethered to the pillar before the Guru began his teaching.

After some years, the Guru passed away. One of his disciples became the new head of that ashram. The practice of tethering the cat to the pillar continued while he taught his disciples. After a few months, the cat died. The next day, when the new Guru began his teachings, he noticed that the cat was missing. He said, 'Don't you know that a cat must be tethered to the pillar here during my teaching? This is our tradition. Please go at once and find a cat for this purpose!' The disciples promptly obeyed his orders. People blindly follow tradition and miss the spirit of tradition.

Some people call themselves as devotees of Lord Krishna. Who was Krishna? He was the personification of joy, happiness and celebration. But, you may have noticed many persons who call themselves devotees of Krishna, go around with a long drawn faces, full of sorrow.

At some stage, devotion turned devoid of love and compassion. Devotion became a dogma.

As people lose touch with feelings and cling to mere words, the whole philosophy of prayer is lost. These days many riots take place in the name of religion; spurred by the absence of an understanding of the essence of religion.

This is not to say that we should not respect traditions established by our forefathers. It is not with a purpose to instigate people against traditions. What is asked is, just this – do all that you do with sacredness, with total involvement, with understanding, and with feelings.

Some people come to me saying, 'We do not have a separate prayer room; there is a noisy factory nearby, the kids are always crying and the wife is always nagging. So, how are we to pray?'

There is absolutely no need for an external peaceful atmosphere for one to pray or meditate. It is possible to pray without mantras and shlokas provided one has peace within.

How is that?

There was an arid open space. Under a scorching sun, work for constructing a temple for Lord Krishna was progressing. Workers were carrying loads of bricks on their heads. A sage who happened to come along asked one of them, 'What are you doing?' and the worker screamed, 'Can you not see? I am carrying bricks!'

The sage asked the same question to another. He said smilingly, 'I am earning a living for my family.'

The sage asked yet another and he replied devotionally, 'I am performing a very sacred task of building a temple for my God.'

As we can see, the actions being same, attitudes are different.

All of us may not be so lucky as to get the job of building a temple; but whatever tasks we perform, if we do that with total involvement like that of building a temple, that itself is the best prayer. God gives us what we need more than what we want.

Reflections

Yoga of Wisdom
Tradition blindly followed kills the spirit of tradition.

Yoga of Action
Don't work for Worship; Work can be Worship.

Contemplation

The most unintelligent of all is a person who refuses to profit from his miseries.

You can't de-mystify the mystery of life.

People blindly follow tradition.

I do not dance because I am happy. I am happy because I dance.

Prayer is not to lighten your burden but to strengthen your back.

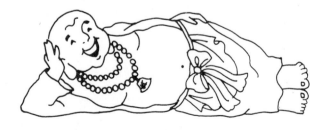

FOR SOME, IT IS A HORRORSCOPE!

Most often, our lives are wasted in fear!

In order to drive away darkness from his house, a foolish person was found carrying out bucket loads of darkness and emptying them. Despite the many years he spent in this task, it was futile. His preoccupation with driving out darkness took him nowhere. Darkness is the absence of light. If only he had attempted to light a small lamp, darkness would have disappeared!

Fear is also similar to darkness. Absence of love is fear! Once the lamp of love is lit, fear would disappear. If you cannot understand this, then let us take an example of love...the love between man and woman. How does this love blossom forth?

Love is born out of the trust between man and woman. Don't you agree? If a man and woman do not trust each other, there can be no love or affection between them.

Reflect on an incident in the life of Mullah Nasruddin, a character in Sufi literature.

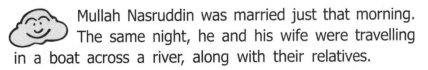 Mullah Nasruddin was married just that morning. The same night, he and his wife were travelling in a boat across a river, along with their relatives.

A sudden storm broke out and the river was turbulent. The boat rocked wildly. Everyone in the boat, including the bride, was in mortal fear. But Mullah remained calm. The bride noticed this and asked in surprise, 'Aren't you afraid?' Mullah, without replying, took out the dagger from his waistband and raised it as though he was going to slit her throat. There was no reaction on her face. He asked, 'Are you not afraid of the dagger?' and she said, 'The dagger may be dangerous, but the person who is holding it, is my loving husband. So I am not afraid.'

'Exactly!' exclaimed Mullah. 'These waves may be dangerous but Allah who is moving them is full of love. So I am not afraid!'

Mullah Nasruddin had faith in Allah. Hence, he was loving and compassionate. Without faith in God, he would have been devoid of love and compassion. Without love and compassion even Mullah would have trembled with fright, just like the others in the boat.

We can apply this example to our lives too! If we are afraid, it only means that we do not trust existence!

We would have come across many who say, 'I am God-fearing!' This is nonsense. We should love God, not fear Him! It should be 'God loving', not 'God fearing!'

Swami Vivekananda said, 'Be fearless. Fearlessness is the message of the Upanishads.'

Some go from one astrologer to another with their horoscopes to find out when death would strike them. As far as they are concerned, their horoscopes are 'horrorscopes.' Such people are more afraid of when they would die rather than what they would do while being alive! This fear would devastate them both mentally and physically!

While talking about mortal fear, Rabindranath Tagore said, 'Long before you were born in this world, compassionately, God made sure that there was milk in both the breasts of your mother. He may well have created another world for you after your death! Who knows? So, have faith!'

We can only advise all those who are afraid...plan for your future; there is no harm in that. But your fear about the future would only ruin your happiness.

In order to protect your wealth, plan where to keep it safe; plan how to insure it against theft and so on! To live in fear, without doing any of these things is meaningless.

Instead of conjuring images of fearful events like 'What if I fail in the examination?', and thus spending time weakening yourself, use it fruitfully to prepare and pass in the examination! Life is a series of examinations; we need to pass them with flying colours. This is a gift we can offer to God.

Reflections

Yoga of Wisdom
Faith does not crave for miracles.
But it often happens miraculously.

Yoga of Action
Faith does not move mountains. But gives
the power to climb one.

WHAT IS HAPPINESS? 1

One day, Mullah was very sad. A close friend who visited him asked, 'Why are you so sad?' In response, Mullah began to cry.

'My maternal uncle died last month - he has bequeathed all his property to me before dying. I thought of that and am crying now!' said Mullah.

'I know your uncle very well!' said the friend, in an attempt to console him. 'He was well over eighty...death is but natural! Why are you so sad for that? In fact, you should feel happy that you got his vast property!'

But Mullah was inconsolable. 'You don't understand my grief, my friend!' he said. 'Only last week, my paternal uncle died, leaving me property worth millions of dollars.' He wept more and was almost uncontrollable.

His friend was really confused. 'I know your paternal uncle too! He was eighty-five...instead of feeling happy that you got so much money, why are you crying like an idiot?' he asked out of irritation.

'My sorrow is worse than that...my grandfather who is over hundred years old died yesterday, bequeathing property worth over 20 million dollars in my name!' cried Mullah.

Now the friend was really fed up. 'I really fail to understand, why at all you should be crying', he asked.

Mullah sniffed, wiped his tears and explained: 'My maternal uncle, paternal uncle and grandfather who were extremely rich are all dead. Now I do not have any more uncles left, to die!'

This tale implies a very important truth. Greed is one of the sources of unhappiness. If we allow it to expand unreasonably, then joy or peace of mind would be the casualty. Happiness and Satisfaction are within us.

Water poured into a cracked pot will not remain in it. Similarly, people without contentment cannot be happy. They will only worry about what they do not possess. Their hearts are always full of sorrow. Once the crack in the pot is sealed, it would hold water poured into it. Similarly, when the blind spots of the mind are removed, it would be filled with joy.

'If I get this and this alone, I would be happy,' declares the mind. This gives rise to many desires. These desires in turn become blind spots.

For some, settling in USA is happiness. For others, getting a visa to go to USA is happiness. It means, 'Until I get my visa, I have postponed being happy.' Yes! pinning their happiness on some event that is likely to happen in the distant future, they let go of the present joys available to them; exactly like a pot with a crack!

Such people with blind spots cannot be really happy even if they do get a visa to go to USA. Because, once they get the visa, they would postpone their happiness by declaring that only when they get a job in USA, they can be happy.

Even if they get a job in USA - will they be happy? No. The desire increases a little more. 'Until I get a green card, there is no happiness!' would be their stand. Once that is achieved, they would declare that there is no joy in the American life; it is only available in India where all their relatives live! Thus, they would again postpone their happiness.

There are other types of people...those who think that happiness is sold in shops. Yes, they appear to be deriving happiness from cigarettes, alcohol, etc.

I am reminded of a story told by Ramana Maharishi when I see such people.

A rich man had a pet dog and took care of it very well. But the dog did not enjoy the meals provided to it. Like any other being, it too wanted a change. It left the house and wandered on the street to look out for its food. It roamed around in vain for days together. It was unable to fight the street dogs. On not having got food even from the garbage and the leaves thrown there with leftover morsels, it came across a dried bone. Being hungry, the dog bit the bone. While chewing the bone, its gum got punctured and blood started oozing out. In the process, the dog thought that the blood was coming out from the bone and started chewing well.

A wise dog looked at it and said, 'Hey! The blood is coming from your gums and not from the bone; it is only a dried bone that you are chewing.' The dog looked at it with disdain and said, 'Until I bit the bone, my tongue had not known the taste of blood! Only after biting this bone, I came to know this taste. So, the blood is coming from the bone. You cannot trick me!'

Saying so, the dog bit the bone more ferociously.

Similarly someone may say 'Before I came in contact with the object I was not happy. After I came in contact with the object, I am happy.... Happiness comes from the object.' This is dog's logic!

Think for a while! Is there any difference between the dog biting the dried-bone and those human beings gaining pleasure from cigarettes and alcohol?

Reflections

Yoga of Wisdom
We are Victims of our Limiting Logic

Yoga of Action
Create the Energy of Rejoicing in what you have rather than Complaining about what you do not have

Contemplation

Where there is trust there is no fear.

I am an optimist. It does not seem too much use being anything else.

..Sir Winston Churchill

The highest knowledge is the knowledge of happiness.

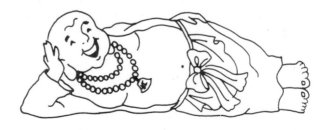

WHAT IS HAPPINESS? 2

A rich man, in order to be happy, went on searching for it, travelling to different countries. He was still not happy. He chased wine, women and other addictions...but his heart was devoid of happiness.

Someone told him that there was happiness in a life of renunciation. So, he decided to try that too. He packed all his wealth, the treasure stored in his house, all diamonds, precious stones, gold ......

He took the bundle and placed it at the feet of a Yogi and said, 'Swamiji! I am placing all my wealth at your feet! I don't need them any more. I only seek peace of mind and happiness! Where is peace?' Saying thus, he fell at the feet of the Yogi in total surrender.

The Yogi did not seem to heed his words at all. He hurriedly opened the bundle and checked the contents. It was full of dazzling diamonds, glittering gold. On viewing these, the Yogi tied up the bundle and ran with it.

The rich man was extremely shocked. 'Oh, no! I have surrendered my wealth to a cheat, a pseudo Godman! What a blunder!' he thought. His sadness turned into anger and he went behind the Yogi in hot pursuit.

The Yogi was unable to run fast. He went into all the lanes and by-lanes, but finally reached the place from where he had started his run...under the tree. The rich man also reached the same place, panting hard. Before he could utter a word, the Yogi said, 'Hey, did you get scared that I would abscond with your wealth? Here, take it! I have no need for it...keep it for yourself!' and returned the bundle to him.

The rich man was very happy that he got back his 'lost' wealth. 'Here is peace', said the Yogi. The Yogi further added, 'You see, all this wealth was with you even before you came here. But you did not derive joy from them. It is the same wealth that is with you now...but you have found a great joy in your heart! So where did the happiness come from ... from wealth or from within you?'

It is clear from the story that joy and happiness are not outside us. They are within us!

The Kingdom of heaven is within you, says the Bible.

Just like the rich man who went roaming around with the bundle of wealth, many of us do not realise this truth. That is the reason why we look up to others for our happiness.

When the boss appreciates our work, 'Good, you did a fine job!' we literally float. When he utters a word of criticism, all happiness deserts us! So we become like a football to be kicked by others.

A drunkard lay down in the street, fully intoxicated and senseless. His friend who happened to come by said to him jokingly, 'Hey, I had gone to your house. I found that your wife has become a widow. So go home quickly and console her!'

The drunkard was very upset. 'Oh, no! My wife has become a widow!' He began to cry. 'How can your wife become a widow when you are alive?' consoled a passer-by. The drunkard answered, 'But my friend told me that my wife has become a widow. He is my close friend and how can I disbelieve him?' The drunkard continued to cry. Our sorrow is similar to that of the drunkard. Even though he experienced sorrow, it was illegitimate as it was born out of ignorance.

In each of us, there is a drunkard. Many things which are not really true make us miserable. At other times, matters which are of no real significance, rob us of our happiness.

Here are some examples:

A young woman was playing with her child on the beach. Suddenly a huge wave dragged the child in. The woman began to wail, 'My baby! My baby is gone!' The God of the seas heard her cry, relented and returned the child alive to the shore. The woman was overjoyed and hugged her child and showered kisses on its cheeks. Glancing at its feet, she noticed that one of the sandals was missing. At once, her joy was shattered and she began to wail again for the missing sandal... 'Oh, one sandal is gone!' This is how we miss seeing the bigger gifts of life; we are lost in petty things.

A farmer had a bumper crop of tomatoes in one season. Yet, the farmer seemed to be very worried. His neighbours enquired of him the reason for his worry. He replied, 'Normally, I feed my pigs with tomatoes.' The neighbours enquired, 'What is the problem? You have a bumper crop this time!', to which the farmer replied, 'Yes. I have a bumper crop; but I do not have a single rotten tomato to offer to my pigs. What will I feed them with?.'

To put it simply, happiness is like a lock, intelligence is like a key. If you turn the key of intelligence in the opposite direction, it would lock up happiness. If you turn it in the right direction, the doors of happiness open!

Reflections

Yoga of Wisdom
The Kingdom of Heaven is within you; do not get lost in the trivial aspects of life.

Yoga of Action
*For every minute you're upset,
you loose sixty seconds of joy.*

Contemplation

Unhappy mind often gives small things a big shadow.

Don't miss seeing the bigger gifts of life.

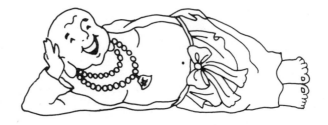

TENSION...TENSION...!

Certain incidents make us so tense...our blood vessels reach a bursting point because of them. Most often, we get so flustered that our limbs begin to tremble! The heart throbs so loudly that a person standing even two feet away can hear it clearly! We experience a fear so strong and inexplicable that it makes us feel as though we were drowning in a dark sea of troubles. All this is due to tension.

Many a time, we get tense on trivialities. Here is an example –

A professor was transferred to another college. In order to see him off, four of his colleagues had come to the railway station with him. As there was still time for departure, the professors standing on the platform, began to chat. They were so engrossed in their conversation that they did not realise that the train had begun to move.

Suddenly flustered, they decided to jump into the train. Without even bothering about which compartment they were getting into, the four of them struggled with the crowd and somehow entered the compartment. Their idea was to move into the correct compartment in the next station.

But one professor holding his luggage in his hands was unable to board the train. A passer-by consoled him saying, 'Don't worry! In another ten minutes the next train would come. You can board that one.'

The professor replied, 'I know that there is another train after ten minutes...I am not worried about myself! I am only worried about my colleagues. They came only to see me off; in the process, they have all boarded the train by mistake!'

This is how tension and agitation make us lose track of even simple matters. When we are agitated, no matter how hard we work to accomplish some task, the net result would just be zero.

Four persons went out to have a drink. All of them got totally drunk. While returning home, it was pitch dark and they had to cross a river. They looked out for the boatman, but he was not to be seen anywhere. The boat was tied to the mooring. They decided to row themselves home. So they got into the boat and began rowing. One hour passed, two hours and then three hours crept by... but they were yet to reach the other side of the bank. Soon it was dawn. Their intoxication was slowly receding. Only then did they notice that the boat was still tied to the mooring!

Just as the drink and darkness blinded the eyes of the drunkards, agitation blinds our minds on several occasions. We are prevented from seeing the truth and reality 'as it is'.

This is a story from Zen Buddhism..

A King wished to select a good Chief Minister for his Kingdom. In his court were four men with equal qualification to hold the post of the Chief Minister. He therefore decided to conduct a test to select one from amongst them for the post.

One day, he called all four of them and said, 'I have a lock. It is a scientific lock, made according to mathematical calculations. Tomorrow morning all of you would be given a chance to open this lock. The person who succeeds in opening this lock within the shortest time would become the Chief Minister of this Kingdom.'

With a desire to become the Chief Minister, the men sat up the whole night, browsing ancient writings regarding locks, mathematical designing etc., and made notes. Only one amongst them looked at a few palm leaves and then went to bed.

The next day, in the king's court, the mathematical lock was brought and placed in front of the four men. The king was also present. The gigantic size of the lock astonished everyone. The four men checked their writings again and again. The men came up, one by one, and looked at the lock. They started referring to their notes about the locks and tried to open the lock. The one who had gone to sleep early was the last one to come. He just came near the lock and inspected it thoroughly. To his surprise, he found the lock was not locked at all! So, without even using a key, this man opened the lock easily by removing the hook. The king appointed him as the Chief Minister. The three others in the anxiety to open the lock did not bother to check whether the lock was locked, in the first place. The fact was, the lock was not locked.

To solve a problem, one must first understand the problem. To understand the problem, the mind should be calm, without tension or agitation. This will facilitate seeing things objectively.

How to be calm?

Just be a witness to your thoughts. Don't identify with them. See them as clouds in the sky of your awareness. Thoughts will come and go; but you don't come and go. You are just a witness. Then the mystery of calmness happens.

Reflections

Yoga of Wisdom
*Life is like a Lock and
Understanding is like a Key.*

Yoga of Action
*Let Alertness be your Inner Guide;
not Tension.*

Contemplation

Be alert and attentive to what a man is and not
to what he has been.

If you are tense you are wrong. If you are joyful
you are right.

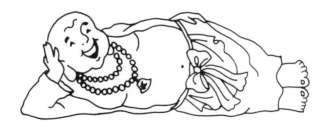

OH, IT IS THE
SAME OLD GIRL!

Before we move on to answer your query as to how to reduce tension, should we not understand how tension is created?

Take a look at this scene -

He has to be in the office at 10 a.m. After a good sleep, when he wakes up in the morning, it is 8 a. m. He has to be in the office within the next two hours. He hurries to the bathroom. The door is closed and his son is inside. 'Are you dozing in there? Come out at once! I have to go to the office!' he screams, and when the son comes out, he goes into the bathroom. There is no toothpaste in its place on the stand. His tension mounts. Somehow he completes his morning rituals and emerges from the bathroom. There is no time for breakfast. He grabs some clothes, wears them and is about to leave for the office. His wife calls out, 'Please take the children with you and leave them in the school on your way!' He gnashes his teeth and takes the kids, leaves them in the school. On reaching the office, he slumps into his seat. His superior asks him for the files that he had attended to on the previous day, and his hands reach into his trouser pocket for the table key...uh,uh! He has forgotten to bring the key! Now his body begins to tremble. So what is the use of his coming to the office in such a hurry?

Now let us see... what is the reason for his tension? Laziness or lack of alertness or lack of planning!

The next major reason for tension is lack of a presence of mind.

God has provided us with eyes and ears. Despite that, very often we do not use these senses and live like blind and deaf people. Above all this, we have an arrogant feeling that we know everything!

Even those who have all the material comforts of life have this shortcoming.

Here is an example - He is a great basketball champion. The college where he studied organizes a celebration in his honour. After the event, he expresses his desire to have a look at his old classroom and the hostel. The college authorities bring him to his old classroom.

Glancing at the room, he exclaims, 'The same old room!' They take him to the hostel – 'The same old hostel!' he quips. The smell of cigarettes lingers in the atmosphere... 'The same old cigarette...' he says. Looking at him approaching his old room in the hostel, one of the college students rushes to the room to warn his roommate who is enjoying a tryst with a co-student. On being warned, this student hides his girlfriend in a cupboard. The champion, who enters the room with the college authorities, looks at the cupboard and says, 'The same old cupboard!' The authorities open the cupboard and the girl jumps out. The champion says automatically, 'The same old girl' and the student screams, 'No, not possible! This is my girlfriend!'

Just brush aside the comedy here and take a deeper look at the meaning behind the story...it reveals that very often, we do not notice the obvious facts which glare at us! Our minds are hijacked by our past and hence not available to the present. Thus, the present is polluted by the past.

If a person is tense, we can without doubt state that the reason for that tension is the person himself more than the circumstances.

One individual cannot perform all the tasks. One has to delegate work to others. One would surely land up in tension if one were to say, 'No one knows how to do these things...I have to do everything!'

Well then, how can we live without tension? What is to be done?

Tension is similar to noise. In order to make a noise, one has to clap one's hands. To live without tension is similar to silence. One cannot create silence. Because, silence is already there.

That is, your effort is required to create tension. To create a situation without tension, your effort is not necessary; only a silent mind is necessary. Your thoughts are nothing but words. Words are noisy. Can your being be wordless? Then see the magic of silence happening in you. This is Meditation.

Reflect on this:

A farmer once came to a Sufi saint with a problem. He said, 'My wife is rearing a lot of cattle and fowl. The whole house is stinking with their odour. I am unable to even breathe. You must show me a way to escape from this nuisance.'

The Saint said, 'Why don't you open the windows? The fresh air would drive out the odour!' and the farmer exclaimed, 'Oh, no! Then my pigeons would fly out of the house!'

Very often, we behave like the farmer when it comes to the tensions that we confront. In order to protect something insignificant like the pigeons, we fail to open the window of wisdom. The result...tension, suffocation. So, let us open wide, the windows of wisdom.

Reflections

Yoga of Wisdom
Be aware of your unawareness.

Yoga of Action
Create an energy of wordless presence; be not a victim to a noisy mind.

Contemplation

Knowledge is often a mask we wear to hide our ignorance.

Let us open wide the windows of wisdom.

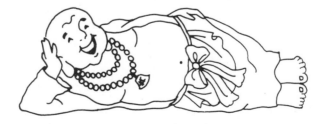

THE SEAGULLS DID NOT COME NEAR THAT DAY!

How is life?

'Somehow it drags on!'

Many of us say 'life drags on' with an expression of utter boredom. If we act with this mental attitude, we would not be able to move even an inch forward in our life. Our life would be bereft of interest or enthusiasm and life without enthusiasm is just aging. How to get out of this quicksand called boredom?

The executives in large corporate companies are taken good care of by their companies and relieved of their boredom or apathy. The company gives them periodical increments or promotions to encourage and motivate them. They provide them with the power and opportunity to take important decisions. Most important of all, they create a feeling in them that they are indispensable to the organisation.

Now consider this...whether it is at home or office, we become indifferent only when our sense of importance diminishes. If others get more attention, we feel jealous. It is this jealousy that builds up the attitude of apathy and lethargy.

'Everyday, it is the same thing! This manager is very annoying!' - this is at the office.

'This bus never arrives on time!' – this is at the bus stop.

'Every time I see your face while going out, nothing turns out right for me!' - this is at home.

It is not the bad manager or the buses that run late that make us feel depressed. The words and expressions that we use to describe the situations are the root cause of our depression. So, if you want to chase away the blues, throw out such words from your everyday vocabulary.

One method to drive away depression and energise ourselves is to employ auto-suggestion!

'Hey, Shankar! You have everything, my boy! You can get this job done better than any one else!' - if we begin to talk to ourselves like this, fresh energy will begin to flow in our minds and bodies. If we become enthusiastic, the light waves that emanate from our bodies would make those around us also enthusiastic.

Does this confuse you? This is a scientifically proven fact!

When we say 'I', there are three factors involved -

- the body
- the mind, and
- the waves or vibrations that emanate from the body.

When we speak of great leaders, we usually say that there is a brightness or aura around them. This aura is from the light waves that emerge from the body of a person.

There is a well-known Zen story about the aura...there was a sage who had realised the truth about himself and the world around him. Everyday he used to sit in front of the ocean and meditate. During those moments, seagulls would fly fearlessly around him and play. At times, these birds would even sit on his shoulders.

One day, as usual, the sage went to the seashore to meditate. A small boy who came to play on the seaside came up to him and said, 'These birds play so freely near you. Won't you catch one and give it to me?'

The sage agreed, thinking that the boy wanted only one bird, and so it was not a big deal. The next day when he went to meditate on the seashore, all the seagulls flew well above his head; not one bird came anywhere near him! The birds were able to sense his intention from the waves that emanated from his body!

Your energy field will also touch people. Make sure you have good energy and create good vibration around you.

One big industrialist I know was in the habit of giving his wife a signed empty cheque book before leaving for work. He had provided her with all the material comforts and almost limitless money. However, every time I visited their home, the wife used to complain 'He never comes home on time! He does not even ask the children about their studies…..'

As far as that lady was concerned, all that she wanted from her husband was that he should sit and talk to her and the children for half-an-hour at least once a week! That was sufficient to make her feel satisfied.

This is known as 'value system' in the study of management. A person designated as 'sales representative' can be highly motivated by a fresh designation as 'sales officer.' This would be more effective than an increment of $ 200.

No matter how enthusiastic we are and however well we motivate our colleagues, even a small failure could dash us down the abyss of depression. There is no denying this fact!

At such times, do keep this in mind - just as the experience of success is sweet, the experience of failure is also sweet. Success has its own flavour; failure has its own flavour too. We can understand this if we learn to view failure as merely postponed success...that is all! There is nothing in it to make us depressed. Treat failure as a fertilizer for success.

Treat each experience as an unique experience. In this wordless experience, your being starts relaxing. Then you will find your life not being a series of vacuums or emotional dungeons.

Reflections

Yoga of Wisdom
*Watch your Aura –
your Energy field, always*

Yoga of Action
*Love promises a safe landing though
not a calm voyage.*

Contemplation

Don't complain too much. The wheel that squeaks the loudest is the one that gets replaced often.

Your energy field will also touch people.

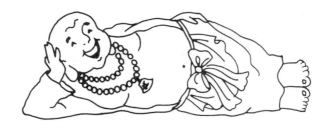

WATCH YOUR THINKING CLOSELY!

𝕯 epression, fear, anger, disgust - where are they generated from?

They are not generated from our hands, legs, lungs or respiratory tubes. They are generated by our thoughts. In that case, what is 'thought'?

Consider this for a minute. When we allow words to flow freely, without moving our lips or tongue, thoughts take shape.

We cannot think without words and sentences. For the time being let us keep aside creative artists like musicians and painters who can think with sounds, colours......

A person starts a business. In the process, he makes a loss. At once he begins to think that he is unfit to do business, he would be unable to understand the nuances of running a business...these very thoughts within his mind would generate a complex feeling. If the same person, on the other hand, tells himself 'Profit or loss is natural in business ...I gain nothing by just getting upset.' These thoughts would enable him to face failure in a positive way and lay a foundation to learn from the failure, as he is open to analyse himself.

This happened during the Second World War.

We are all aware that the Nazis conducted gruesome experiments on prisoners of war. This was one such experiment - they told the prisoners, 'We are going to kill you in a novel way! We want to see how you die when blood in your body is slowly drained away.'

As a trial, they put two prisoners in bed and began to drain their blood. The blood was allowed to drain into a nearby bottle making a dripping sound. After a few minutes, they tied their eyes with a black cloth. Then they stopped draining the blood from one of the prisoners' body. But the dripping noise was made to continue, using some other means. The prisoner who was listening to the sound began to tremble in mortal fear. He thought that all the blood was draining from his body, while in reality, it was not so.

'Oh, I am going to die in a short while...!' was his thinking. By the end of the experiment, both the prisoners died.

In the case of the first prisoner, the very feeling of his blood oozing out continuously was sufficient to kill him. The reason for his death was his mere thoughts impacting his feelings.

We need to understand the simple matter with respect to the statements we make as follows:

'It is so boring!'

'I am so tired!'

'I feel so ill!'

'Is this a child? It is a demon...'

Avoid using such readymade negative statements. This must be avoided not only while speaking, but also while thinking within oneself.

Now what I have been explaining so extensively can be condensed into one word - 'language.'

To start with, there is no need to control or curb our thoughts; good or bad. Let our thoughts run for a while, taking the natural course. What is important is to watch our thoughts very carefully; followed by the kind of words we use to express our thoughts. In a way, this is a basic quality required for meditation.

Let the awareness be alive to practice this again and again; whenever there is an opportunity. This will remove the readymade negative language that we normally use.

With continuous practice, stimulating and self-motivating thinking would become a part of us in the natural course of time.

We can make an attempt to be in-charge of our thoughts and emotions. What do we do when others make us angry by abusing and humiliating us?

Let us see how to handle this dimension.....

Reflections

Yoga of Wisdom
Thoughts can make you;
thoughts can break you

Yoga of Action
No person is so poor that he can not talk
to himself positively.

BEYOND POSITIVE THINKING!

When someone expresses his anger towards us, or speaks in a belittling way, what should we do? The answers to such questions can be found in this incident from the life of the Buddha.

Once Buddha went to beg with his disciple Ananda. When they approached a house for food, the lady of the house spoke harshly. 'You lazy fellows! You are hale and hearty...why can't you work for your food?' she yelled and chased them away. The disciple was enraged at the woman that she used such hostile words on his great Guru.

'Please permit me to teach that woman a solid lesson...' he pleaded with Buddha. But Buddha walked away in silence.

A little later, Buddha handed over his water container to Ananda and went to take rest.

Having rested for a couple of hours they resumed their journey. On the way, Buddha glanced at the water container and asked, 'Whose is this?' 'It is yours, Guruji!' said Ananda. Buddha took it and looked at it once and returned it to Ananda saying, 'No, I gifted it to you a little while ago...it is yours.'

At night, Buddha pointed to the same water container and asked once again, 'Whose is this?' Now Ananda said, 'Guruji, it is mine!'

Hearing this, Buddha said laughingly, 'I asked you the same question earlier this evening and you said it was yours. Now you are saying, it is mine. How can the same container be yours and mine at the same time?'

Though Ananda was slightly confused, he replied calmly, 'Guruji, you said that you have gifted this container to me and I accepted it. Hence, I said that it was mine. Initially, when you gave it to me I did not consider it as mine, because, even though you had handed over the container to me, it was still yours!'

Buddha smiled at Ananda and said, 'Similarly, I did not take the words the lady spoke harshly as mine; I did not accept them. So, even though the words were spoken at me, they still belong to the lady alone. That is the reason I said that there was no need to teach her a lesson.'

This advice from Buddha to his disciple expounds a very simple truth.

If someone calls us 'lazy' we get affected by that word only when we take it to be ours. If we are clearly and firmly aware that we are not lazy, what that person says about us is just nonsense. 'Nonsense' would never affect us. In fact, we would not pay any heed to a person who speaks nonsense!

If someone calls me lazy and I am deeply affected, it only reflects on my true nature of being lazy. The quality in me is pointed out by others. This is the root cause for getting affected. This gives rise to blood pressure and tension.

Now let us assume that a person is indeed very lazy. Would it be possible for him to change? Of course, there would be a possibility! Take a look at this story...

There was a very successful businessman. He lived in plenty and prosperity. Unfortunately, his ship got caught in a storm and sank. His factory was closed down due to labour trouble. His debts exceeded his assets and he lost everything in the process and became a pauper. For five long years, he worked very hard and gained back his lost status; constructed a bigger factory; acquired not one, but two ships; now he was richer than ever before! Learning about this turn of fortune, journalists came to interview him. They flooded him with questions about the secret of his success. His reply to them was, 'I know that I failed in my business... but I never told myself that I am a failure ......that is the reason behind my regained success!' Failing in an endeavour is one dimension and to treat oneself as a failure is yet another dimension.

This story could be an eye-opener to many.

You may feel lazy... lethargic and lose interest in work. But for heaven's sake do not label yourself 'lazy' or 'good-for-nothing.' If you do that, you will become your own worst enemy, and prevent yourself from becoming successful.

Well then, in that case, what should one do?

Tell yourself 'I am not lazy' is the solution given by some. This is known as 'Positive Thinking.' But what I have to say here may be a little shocking to some of you. The truth is; 'positive thinking' would not serve you in the long run.

Reflections

Yoga of Wisdom
*More than the fact, it is the
interpretation of the fact that hurts*

Yoga of Action
*The quality of your life is the quality of
your communication to yourself.*

Contemplation

Most of us are lazier in mind than in body.

The quality of your life is the quality of your self-talk.

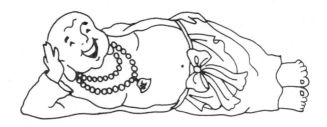

DO NOT CLOSE THE DOORS OF YOUR THINKING!

Whenever depression, low self-esteem, etc., raise their ugly heads within us, it is a good idea to boost ourselves by telling 'I am born to be successful, I am a great achiever' and so on. This would produce temporary results, but in the long run, such positive thinking alone would not suffice.

It is similar to the advice to chant 'Rama, Rama', every time that a bad thought arises in our minds. Positive thinking is also based on the same philosophy. When we are tormented by temptations, repeatedly chanting the names of Gods would certainly help to divert these temptations. But, the temptations may arise repeatedly. Should one chant *Rama nama* again to control such thoughts?

Say for example, the whole house is stinking...due to a dead rat. We do not have the time or patience to go hunting for the dead rat and throw it out. So, we light up incense sticks to camouflage the bad smell. It would cover that smell for a while. But, once the incense burns out, the same rotten smell would again pervade the atmosphere.

Positive thinking is similar to this. Is there a better alternative to positive thinking? There is - and that is known as Authentic Thinking.

Let us assume that you are in deep trouble. Instead of lamenting 'Oh, God! My thoughts are always revolving around my troubles...' one can turn to the philosophy of positive thinking. Then one may say to oneself, 'No, I am really happy!' and try to thrust this thinking into one's mind. This would create a conflict within the mind. It would however not help resolve the trouble. Instead, try to view your thinking from a distance... similar to a bird's eye view.

Without labelling your thoughts as 'good' or 'bad', without showing any aversion to your thoughts, take an impartial stand and notice your thoughts. This is called as seeing things through a bird's eyes.

Whether the thoughts are sad, tempting or happy; without identifying them with yourself, when you view them from a distance, a clear understanding will crystallize within you.

Once this mental state is attained, sadness and happiness will appear as two sides of the same coin. Happiness is an experience. Similarly, sadness is also another experience. For people who do not have peace of mind and clarity, even happiness will appear as an experience of sadness!

A father belonging to a middle class family, had six daughters. They were all of marriageable age. Just worrying about their marriage, he suffered a heart attack. He was admitted to a hospital. There was news of his winning a million dollars in a lottery on the same day. His wife worried as to how to break this good news during this crisis. She requested the doctor's help.

The doctor undertook the task by using psychological methods. He slowly asked him, 'What would you do if you win $ 100,000 in a lottery?'

The patient replied that he would get his eldest daughter married. The doctor continued, 'If you get $ 200,000?'

He said, 'I shall get the second daughter also married!'

'All right! If you get $1,000,000?' the doctor asked.

'Oh, come on doctor! Where will I get the lucky chance? In case that happens, definitely I will give you $300,000!' promised the patient.

This unexpected happy news precipitated a heart attack for the doctor himself and he died!

Just as happiness is one kind of taste, sorrow is also another taste. This philosophy may be difficult to accept. When I was a little boy, I used to watch my mother eating bitter gourd with relish. I was then quite confused as to how she could really enjoy eating something so bitter. But once the heart takes to it, even bitterness can be enjoyable. I later understood that just as sweetness could be enjoyable, bitterness also can be enjoyable. Every taste has its own flavour.

Children feel sweetness is the only good taste. They conclude tastes such as bitterness, sourness, etc., cannot be good and avoid them. This is also a similar situation. We assume that only happiness is desirable and all other feelings are not; we close the doors of our thinking to most of our feelings.

When one views thinking in its purest form; authentically and objectively seeing one's thoughts and feelings, but not identifying with them, then the mind automatically becomes calm. Truths are revealed; barriers break down. Life will blossom like a beautiful flower - softly, gently and silently!

Reflections

Yoga of Wisdom
*Don't be a Victim of an Experience;
but be a Victor.*

Yoga of Action
Experience the experience of what is.

Contemplation

An open mind understands an empty one.

One can always tell a failure by the way one critisizes success.

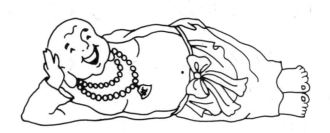

A CANDLELIGHT THAT HID THE MOONLIGHT!

*T*here was an egoistic king. Once when he went to the forest to hunt, he met a sage. The sage was meditating with his eyes closed. The king said, 'I have won over many lands and have annexed them to my kingdom. My treasury overflows with riches that I have brought from various places. In my palace, there are many wonderful and pretty women from different regions, ready to please me. Yet I am not happy. When will I become happy?'

The sage, opening his eyes, screamed at him, 'You will be happy only when I die!' and closing them again, went back to meditation.

In a rage, the king drew out his sword to kill him, saying, 'I am a great king! How dare you insult me thus?' The sage opened his eyes again and said, 'Hey you fool! I did not mean myself when I said 'I.'..I meant the ego. When the ego dies, you will be happy!'

If a person who has less education, status or wealth expresses an opinion contrary to our own, we do not accept it. It is our ego which does not permit us to accept the same. We immediately react negatively.

Consider this a little more deeply. An egoistic person expects others to listen to his point of view. 'Every one should show respect to me!' would be his stand and expectation. What does that mean? He would be happy only if others show him respect. Simply said, in order to feel happy, he expects others to nod their heads in agreement with him. He is like a beggar indirectly begging others to show him respect. When others do not give him the alms of 'respect', his peace of mind is lost and happiness disappears!

Hindu scriptures mention God as 'Ananda' meaning 'joy.' The word ego could be expanded thus - **E**dging **G**od **O**ut - that means, moving God or joy away from us is the state of ego.

In Hindu tradition, people break coconuts in front of God to symbolize breaking of ego. While breaking the coconut, we indirectly signify to ourselves, 'Oh, God! I am breaking the ego - 'I', in front of you!'

Just as sweet water comes out of the broken coconut, so does joy emerge when ego is surrendered.

Let us say that you happen to state your opinion among friends or in the work place. Your emphasis on the opinion is quite strong. Yet, somehow your idea is not accepted. If you were a person without ego, you would not worry too much about it. Whether others praise your idea, or make fun of it, accept it or reject it, you would not be unduly affected.

Reflect on this story:

This is an incident from the life of Tagore. Once he was crossing the river Yamuna by boat. It was night. Under candlelight, Tagore tried to compose a poem. But somehow, the poetry would not flow. Finally, he gave up and put off the candle. The moment the candlelight went off, moonlight filled the boat and the boat appeared beautiful! Tagore experienced a great sense of beauty. At once, poetry began to flow out of his heart... effortlessly!

What is the connection here? The candlelight was capable of hiding the moonlight! In the same way, petty ego hides the vast happiness of heart.

Reflections

Yoga of Wisdom
*Do not be trapped in the
tradition of ego; but purify it.*

Yoga of Action
*Attitude of ego-lessness creates
altitude of joy.*

HOW TO HANDLE A NAGGING WIFE / HUSBAND?

𝕴 was at Madras to deliver a speech on labour relations. In that session, many top executives raised queries about unions, labour problems .... After the session, only one person in a dark suit remained in his chair. Ensuring that no one else was around, he began to speak.

'Swamiji! My work involves managing five thousand workers and five labour unions. Be it a canteen problem or bonus issue, I am the one who settles the matter! So normally I am the first one to enter the office and by the time I return home, it is generally late in the night. Due to this, I have to face a lot of trouble at home. My wife nags me saying, 'Why have you got married, when you cannot attend to the needs of the family?' I am unable to tolerate her chiding. If I take the trouble to run the company efficiently, to get a good name, good income, promotion to a better position .... Doesn't it mean that she too gains a better living and status? But she does not seem to understand any of this! I will bring her to you...you should give her some sound advice.'

I told him of cases where a few women complain 'My husband is at home within half an hour after the office

87

closes. Our children are all grown up. It is very embarrassing to see my husband hanging around me all the time, even at this age!'

I have to say this because no woman wishes that her husband should spend all the time with her, from morning to night! All that a wife needs is 'quality time' and not 'quantity time.' You are a busy executive. Even if you talk to your wife for just ten minutes while eating, it is sufficient. But, during those ten minutes, you should not think about your work place. Open your eyes and look at your wife... not just dutifully. Do remember how you used to look at her when you two were newly weds? With great eagerness and desire! Once the husband begins to enjoy the good looks of his wife, then where is the chance for her to crib?

'It is not just enjoying her looks...if you notice that she has changed her hair style, appreciate that! If the breakfast is good, praise - say, 'No one can prepare breakfast the way my wife does!' But do not make it sound like an insincere or hollow praise. Make it authentic and real. Discover her good attributes and praise her whole-heartedly.

'Now, do not ask me, 'Where is the need for such flattery between husband and wife?' In that case, where is the depth of a relationship?' This is not flattery, this is genuine praise.

'Even prayer to God is known as 'Sthuti' in our land. Sthuti means praise. When God can be pleased with Sthuti, why not your wife enjoy praise as she is an ordinary mortal?

'The main reason for your wife's complaint is that of getting your attention. It means that she feels that you belong to her; she is not willing to give you up totally for your office work alone. Each individual has to fulfil multiple roles in life. In fact, you must be really proud of having such a loving wife!'

Finally I said, 'Follow the methods I told you. If none of them work, then begin to enjoy the nagging of your wife.'

The ability to enjoy everything is a quality of an awakened consciousness. Your commitment to enjoy should be above your likes and dislikes.

The man left in total confusion only to return a week later. He said, 'Swamiji! What you told me is really true! After following your advice, the two of us had a one to one chat without any hostility after many, many years! Thank you!'

Vatsyayana in his Kamasutra speaks about the relationship between husband and wife. It may sound strange - but this is how he explains it.

The relationship between husband and wife begins in sex. The ultimate goal of a married relationship should flower into compassion. I call this ladder of love as the incremental growth in relation between husband and wife.

Sex ➤	Love ➤	Friendliness ➤	Devotion ➤	Compassion
⅄	⅄	⅄	⅄	⅄
Lust ➤	Caring ➤	Non-domination ➤	Sacredness ➤	Forgiveness

From the above, it can be seen that the centre of sex is lust. The centre of love is caring. The centre of friendliness is non-domination. The centre of devotion is sacredness. The centre of compassion is forgiveness.

The relationship between a husband and wife begins in lust. The next stage is caring - they feel for each other. The third stage is the friendship that blossoms between the two. In pure friendship, persons can remain in equality. They would not feel that one is inferior to the other. They would not plot to ruin each other. There is no domination of one over the other.

When friendship develops between the husband and wife, both of them would cherish their relationship as something sacred; they would protect the relationship!

The final stage in this relationship is compassion. The basis of compassion is forgiveness. Whether it is the husband or wife, it is but natural, mistakes do happen. Forgiving mistakes made by the other is the last and highest stage of the relationship. Only at this level, does relationship become complete.

Can you transform your sexual relationship into a sacred relationship? In this process a spiritual intimacy will develop. If your relationship has forgiving quality, then you don't bug each other but lovingly hug each other. Only in this space, is a relationship fulfilling.

Reflections

Yoga of Wisdom
*Distinguish between the usefulness of
Quality Time and Quantity Time.
Understand the ladder of Love.*

Yoga of Action
Learn to see Elegance in what is and Express it.

Contemplation

Ego is – 'Edging God Out'.

A shallow man is one who is full of oneself.

Transform sex into prayer.

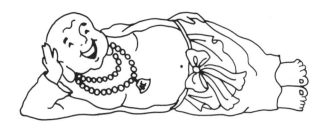

WITH FOLDED HANDS AND CLOSED EYES...

God has given us one mouth and two ears so that we speak less and listen more. But for most of us the sweetest sound on earth is our own voice! That is why many speak non-stop, whether required or not.

In oriental philosophy as well as our forefathers' prescriptions, importance has been given to 'listening' . In order to listen to others, we must stop speaking. But, we do not; do we?

A lady closed her eyes, folded her hands and began to pray to Mother Mary. Her lengthy prayer was nothing but a list of 'wants.'..it dragged on as 'I want this...I want that...' and so on.

The famous painter Michaelangelo was deeply involved in his work. He heard the voice of the lady pestering the Lord. Just for fun, he hid behind a pillar and said, 'My girl, I am greatly enamoured by your devotion! I am Jesus Christ. What is it that you want?' The lady, in turn, replied in irritation, 'Jesus, please keep quiet! I am talking to your Mother Mary; not to you. Don't disturb!' If a person is eager to speak, even divine intervention cannot deter that urge.

Some people talk endlessly merely to derive pleasure. When one stops talking, and listens to others, the importance of what others have to say will be understood. But the interpretation of what one listens to is also important.

Buddha addressed a gathering; 'Do not forget to complete your duties before going to sleep.' The disciples meditated before their sleep. A thief also heard Buddha's sermon. He was a professional thief. He asked himself, 'What is my duty? I am a thief, my duty is to rob. Buddha has endorsed my life style.' Interpreting like this, he continued to rob everyday before he went to sleep.

Each one listens to one's own chattering mind.

In the Holy Bible, there is a phrase 'silly Christ.' The word 'silly' has a totally different meaning today. But during Biblical times, it meant 'innocent.' If we understand that ancient phrase in today's meaning, just think what pain it would cause to the concerned persons!

Very often we do not listen to the ideas of others with an open mind. 'Who is speaking? What is his objective? Why does he talk on such matters in these circumstances?' - such deep analysis is necessary while we listen to others. Many do not have this maturity to objectively listen. They are not willing to accept what others speak.

It is only now, that western scholars have begun to lay emphasis on the importance of listening. But this matter has been discussed in Hinduism several thousands of years ago!

The purpose of depicting Lord Ganesha with huge ears is to show that he listens carefully and attentively to the words of others.

We may well ask, what is the evidence for this statement. The whole depiction of the body of Lord Ganesha denotes how a human being should be and what characteristics he should possess.

The huge belly of the Lord has a specific meaning. One is faced with a lot of problems in this worldly life. The God's stomach denotes that one should learn to stomach and digest all the problems of life and overcome them.

The trunk of Lord Ganesha shows that one must develop skills. This large limb is capable of picking up even a tiny needle from the ground. At the same time, it is also capable of uprooting a tall tree!

The broken tusk of the Lord reveals one should master one's likes and dislikes. Our likes and dislikes are like ivory; very valuable. Broken tusk represents operating from commitment; not from likes and dislikes. The small axe in his hand is the tool, which says that human beings should cut away their desires and infatuations.

The mouse at the feet of Lord Ganesha is waiting for orders from the Master. Here the mouse is likened to 'desires.' The offerings − fruits & eatables − induce temptation, but the mouse (desire) is only waiting for orders from the Master − the Lord. Desire should be one's servant; not master.

We can continue to expound on the figure of Ganesha and its underlying meanings.

Do make sure that all these concepts do not enter through one ear and go straight out through the other! Let your intellect discern what is right and what is not. What I have tried to convey with the help of Michaelangelo, Lord

Ganesha and Buddha has been put in a nutshell by Sage Thiruvalluvar (Tamil Saint) in just one and three-quarter lines...

Whoever or whatever said it, it is wise to grasp the truth from it no matter who said it. (Kural 423)

Reflections

Yoga of Wisdom
*God has given us two ears and
one mouth – listen more and talk less*
— *Mark Twain*

Yoga of Action
*You can win more friends with your ears
than with your mouth.*

Contemplation

*There are two types of boring people –
those who talk too much and
those who listen too little.*

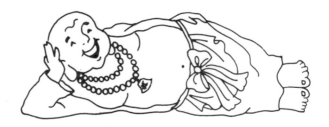

IT WAS THE FAULT OF RIVER GANGA!

I have the opportunity to travel far and wide and the occasion to meet people from different cultures. Most foreigners speak with a sense of wonder about India's rich spirituality, natural wealth, the unity maintained in spite of the cultural diversity and so on. They also ask me how despite such a rich heritage, our nation has not attained material wealth? I have maintained discreet silence without answering the question. I do ask myself this question but the answer turns out to be 'we-know-everything-attitude.' This is my honest opinion.

When we operate with an attitude of 'I know everything', we fail to consider even those issues unknown to us. The simple reason is, we cannot be open minded as we come from a structure 'we-know-everything.'

'Many of us remain blind and deaf despite having eyes and ears', Jesus said. That is why our country remains in poverty inspite of having all riches. There is a story about this.

There was an excellent student. He had learnt many things from expert masters. He wanted to learn about the river Ganga. So he went about meeting many scholars who knew a lot about the river...he spent many days in gathering various details....... where the river originates, runs narrow, runs wide, where it gets flooded, where it mingles with tributaries .....

After obtaining all possible details, he prepared an elaborate map featuring the river Ganga. Now he was quite sure that he knew everything that was to be known about the river. With that attitude, he got into a boat at Rishikesh. He wanted to reach the Bay of Bengal by boat, where the river merges with the ocean. The map matched with the riparian flow - exactly; turning and twisting in all the right places. Now the student was intoxicated with his own knowledge and felt extremely proud that he knew the whole history of the river. Suddenly, the river took a left turn. According to his map, it should have turned to the right. The student was shocked. But he was unable to accept that the map could be wrong. He wanted the river to follow the map. He turned furious with the river. He broke his journey half way through and returned home. Since he acted from the mentality that 'I-know-everything-attitude', he was not able to fully experience and enjoy the mysteries of the river.

We create maps of people and want people to fit in to our maps. We are too stuck with the map and hence miss the joy of being with the people.

Another bad habit we possess is the inability to correct our errors easily. Though we know that the mistake is ours, we justify our actions. The bigger joke is in considering ourselves very clever for being able to justify our mistakes effectively! This mentality is called as being a 'smart Alec' or 'smartie'!

A hawker was selling hand fans made of palm leaves. He proclaimed 'This fan is long lasting, it will last for one hundred years. So the price is $5..' The king who saw this from his balcony was amused. He called the man into the palace and said, 'Hey, are you joking? How can this flimsy fan cost $5? It should not cost even one cent! On top of it, you say it will last for 100 years. What a bluff?'

The Hawker said, 'Oh King, this is a very rare fan. It can last for one hundred years. That is why the price is so high!' The king refused to accept his explanation; but the hawker went on pursuing. Finally the King gave up. The King agreed to buy a fan on the condition that if it failed to last a hundred years, he would cut the hawker's head off!

Later, as expected, the fan tore within a few hours.

The king's men went looking for the hawker and brought him to the palace. The king ordered him to be killed. The hawker said, 'Oh, King! I am not afraid to die. But I really wonder how this fan that should have lasted one hundred years, tore within such a short time in your hands! So, before killing me, would you be kind enough to explain to me how you used it?'

The King relented to his last wish and showed him how he used the fan. At this, the hawker exclaimed with a hurt look,

'Oh, no! This is where the whole mistake is! This fan would surely last for one hundred years...but this is not the way to use it. One should keep the fan in front and shake one's face to and fro and not the fan.... Then the fan would last for 100 years.'

We are experts in justifying our follies.

Now can you understand what being a smart Alec means?

Reflections

Yoga of Wisdom
One is an expert in rationalising one's fallacies.

Yoga of Action
*See what is, 'as is'; what is not, 'as is not'.
Then you will find a priceless treasure.*

Contemplation

We create maps and want people to fit into our maps.

We are experts in justifying our follies.

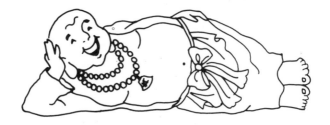

KAIZEN - CONTINUOUS IMPROVEMENT

Shall I tell you about the various principles followed by people of prosperous countries in order to develop their nations further?

The people of the West have a certain approach towards prosperity. Once they set their goal to get a crop of two thousand apples per acre, they would toil relentlessly to reach that goal. They would not worry about the fertility of the land, whether it can give such produce, and so on. They would somehow manage to reach that crop level, even if they had to use chemical fertilizers. This approach is known as Result-Oriented Management.

The approach of the Japanese people however, is slightly different. They would not be so keen as to how many apples grew in one acre. Instead, they would concentrate on the methodology of cultivating apples. 'In what type of soil can apples be cultivated...how often should the plants be watered...' Their whole attention would be on such matters concerned with the cultivation of apples. This approach is known as Process-Oriented Management.

The quantity of apples grown per acre by the Japanese may at times even be less than that grown by the West. But the apples cultivated by them would be tastier.

This approach of the Japanese is similar to the essence of Bhagavad Gita... 'Do your duty without worrying only on the results – the result is interwoven in the very act itself.'

The backbone of Japanese' success is the principle known as Kaizen. Do you know the meaning of this term? It means, 'continuous improvement.' That is to say, no matter how well a job is done; the next time it should be done even better than the previous time.

Just as we greet each other with a 'Namasthe!' or 'Good Day', the Japanese say 'victory to the river of life!' For the Japanese, victory is not a goal...they view each passing moment as a success. For them, life itself is a victory.

When two people compete or fight, one person wins and the other loses...isn't that so? Can both win?

They can! This is known as a 'Win-Win' approach. Take the example of a company. Two executives are discussing about a problem. One expresses his opinion about the solution while the other's opinion is exactly opposite. Both of them are drawn into a heated argument. In this argument, if one wins, the other should lose. But, on the other hand, let us assume both of them view their opinions focusing on the solution to the problem without bothering who is right and who is wrong... then they would reach a conclusion. The focus should be let both win; in such a space a different energy opens up. This very process will make them happy and satisfied. In such a situation, both of them would feel as if they have won. This is Win-Win approach. This method is extensively used today by Indian corporates.

People generally operate from

- I win, you lose - Then you are always in conflict with the other.

- You win, I lose - You start feeling low over a period of time.

- You lose, I lose - This is a sick attitude

- I win, you win - A healthy attitude

- No lose approach - If I win, I win; If I lose, I learn; therefore, I win (in other words, if I win, I rejoice my winning, if I lose I learn from it. So one can always be a winner, if one has this attitude).

'I am keen to succeed. I have the necessary skills and capabilities. But my colleagues do not allow me to come up. They suppress me and prevent me from succeeding...' is a common cribbing we hear often. What I say may be difficult to digest. But please listen.

If a person is really keen to succeed, even if someone hinders, he would still come up, like a buried plant sprouting from the ground. Even if a burning torch is held downwards, its flame is sure to rise up towards the sky!

One does not seek the opinion of a tree to decide whether it is a good tree or bad tree. It is known from the fruit that is borne by the tree. Similarly, the world would not wait to find out whether you are a person born to achieve great things in life after asking your opinion about that! It would be revealed by itself; by weighing your achievements!

Have an attitude of 'I will better my best.' Then an unknown power in you will arise. Meet people with 'win-win' attitude and 'no-lose' approach. You will find a mysterious power within.

Reflections

Yoga of Wisdom
While climbing the tree, grip the branches not the flowers.

Yoga of Action
Our goal should not be only success; but success and service.

Contemplation

*God creates opportunities
but expects us to search for them.*

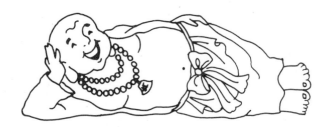

A PROBLEM OR AN OPPORTUNITY?

℣roblem**!!**'

This is one of the many negative words that we use very regularly in our daily conversation. 'Problem in the workplace...problem at home...what a life?'

What is a problem?

Look at this incident. A young graduate was tired of hunting for a job. After many years, he got a job as a journalist. He went to the office full of expectations and a subtle fear. The chief editor called him and said, 'Today is Independence day. A navy vessel has docked in our harbour. Navy personnel are celebrating Independence day on that vessel. Cover this as a news item for our magazine.'

First day, first assignment!

The young man ran excitedly towards the harbour. In the evening, the other reporters who went to various places like the fort, collectorate, party office and so on, gathered in the main office to give finishing touches to their respective reports. The new journalist was alone, sitting soulfully, without writing anything. One of his colleagues asked him gently, 'Why aren't you writing your report'?

'It is all my luck! When I try to sell flour, a high wind blows and when I go to sell salt, it rains! The very first day, my assignment has got me into trouble. The editor sent me to cover Independence Day celebrations on the Navy vessel. There were no celebrations on that vessel', the young journalist expressed sardonically.

'Why?' pursued the colleague.

'There was a big hole in that vessel. People who had gathered there were busy in the preparations; hence no one noticed it. Only when a lot of water had entered the vessel, did someone notice it. And thereafter, they were busy repairing the vessel. How on earth could they celebrate Independence day?' asked the new journalist sulkily.

His colleague was excited. He exclaimed, 'My God! That news should come on the first page!' and ran out to collect further information on that mishap.

The very information that made the new journalist wilt in sorrow because he viewed it as a 'problem', was a golden opportunity for the other to prove his talent. The new journalist had missed an opportunity, which was spotted by another reporter.

Life is not something that happens according to a planned agenda. It is a procession of unexpected opportunities! In fact, each problem is an opportunity for us.

Buddha was walking through a forest. The woodcutters who were cutting wood nearby ran to him and said, 'Stop, please stop! There is a terrible demon in the forest. He is a cannibal who eats human flesh! After eating a person, he cuts off the thumb and keeps it safe. In that way, he has so far collected 999 thumbs. He needs just one more to make it 1000. His plan is, once the final thumb is collected, to string them all up and wear them around his neck! So, please do not go into the forest. If you go, it would be a big problem for you!'

To that, Buddha replied, ' I would get no better opportunity than this!' and entered deep into the forest.

As expected, the demon felled a huge branch of a Banyan tree and appeared in front of Buddha in a cloud of dust. But Buddha did not run away like others in fright. He stood strong, firm and said, 'If killing me gives you pleasure, you may please do so! I accept the fact that you are really strong. But one thing...though you have the strength to break a branch of a Banyan tree, you can never attach it back to that tree. It is very easy to destroy...but very difficult to join!'

'You know the art of destroying, I know the art of joining!', Buddha replied.

More than his words, the truth and compassion touched the demon deeply. After that, he became a disciple of Buddha. He was Anguli Mala.

Let us not go into the analysis of the story. The truth of the tale is very simple. The demon was not a 'problem' for

Buddha; instead it was an opportunity to protect the villagers from further misery. That is all!

For some, even small matters appear to be giant problems. I met one such person recently at Madras.......

Reflections

Yoga of Wisdom
Opportunity is 'Now Here' or 'No where'!

Yoga of Action
Ability is the Alertness to cash in on the Opportunity.

Contemplation

You know the art of destroying,
I know the art of joining!

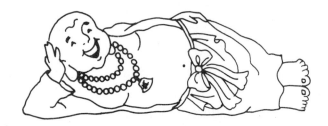

LIFE ENDED
ON THE FIRST NIGHT!

*T*here are many who view even a small matter through a magnifying glass and get terrified.

Recently I had been to Madras to conduct a training programme on self-development called LIFE (Living in Freedom, an Enquiry).

On the first day of the programme, a woman approached me and said, 'My son refuses to listen to anything that I say. If this continues, he may not even marry the girl I choose for him!'

'All right! Please bring your son tomorrow...I shall speak to him,' I said sympathetically.

'Oh, no, Swamiji! Please advise him right now!' said the woman, placing her five-year-old son in front of me!

I was unable to control my laughter!

That little boy was refusing to eat...he was drawing pictures when asked to write 'A...B...C.' Her question was, as he was not obeying her in such trivial matters presently, how could she expect him to listen to her words when he grew up into adulthood? This far-sighted fear was her problem!

There are also other types of people...those who do not stop at viewing the problem with fear; but also magnify it out of proportion. It is like, a monkey which, when bruised, does not leave the bruise alone. It continues to scratch till the bruise turns into a big wound; some even die from such wounds.

Reflect on this!

A couple were just married ....and it was their first night together. The husband wanted to share his experience, somewhat like a confession. He began like this 'When I was young and in college, I used to drink with my friends. But from today onwards...' he was not even allowed to complete his sentence. The new bride simply opened the bedroom door and walked out.

'You have got me married to a drunkard...my life is ruined!' she screamed at the parents. The husband who was watching this scene was so filled with shame that he ran away, not only from the house, but also from the town itself!

There are yet another type of people. They willingly put themselves into highly problematic situations. Here is one such example.

There was a well-to-do businessman from Pune. He was facing financial crisis due to loss in his trade. He volunteered to take me in his car after one of my programmes and I agreed. It was summer and sultry. I felt too hot inside; and started lowering the window glass. Immediately he stopped me as though I was touching a live-wire. Unable to understand his behaviour, I asked for the reason. He replied, 'Swamiji! this place is full of my relatives. If we lower the window pane of the car, they would guess that I don't have air-conditioning in my car! So, please bear with me until we pass through some distance.'

In the process, both of us were suffocating inside the car only to brandish his vanity among his relatives. Vanity prevailed over comfort!

It is true that we may face problems at times, in our lives, unlike the aforesaid examples. During such moments, there are two possible ways out for us. One, catch the bull by the horn and directly confront a problem. We may come over the problem or the problem could overcome us!

Well, how to overcome a problem?

Let us see a simple comparison here...confronting a problem is similar to dating. Oh, don't get flustered that I am using a 'Bad term'; now, what is dating?

It is simply an attempt by a young man or woman to find out about the tastes, likes and dislikes of a person of the opposite sex...is it not?

View the problem like someone who is beautiful and try to 'date.' You will soon get to know the full dimensions of the problem, the ways and means to tackle it, and so on!

Do not consider the problem as a punishment. You will definitely suffer. Take it as a challenge, you will feel energized!

Reflections

Yoga of Wisdom
We major on minor things

Yoga of Action
*Learn to convert challenges into choices.
Failure in life is, who lives but
fails to love.*

CAT .... WHAT PRICE?

A lady said, 'I had been married for several years and was childless. So, I took a vow to visit Tirupati (the richest temple in India, situated in the State of Andhra Pradesh) and tonsure my head, to beget a baby.' Later I became pregnant and gave birth to a baby. Just as I was planning to visit Tirupati, my sister's marriage was fixed. Now I was in a dilemma... how could I attend my sister's marriage with a tonsured head? In Tirupati, I just offered a few hairs to fulfil my vow instead of a full tonsure. Is it right or wrong? Now I feel very guilty about the whole thing! Will this affect the baby in some way?'

To which, I narrated a story. There was a very rich man. After visiting many countries for trade, he was returning home. As the ship reached the mid ocean, there was a storm. The wind was blowing very strong and the mighty waves rocked the ship. The man was terrified! He prayed in desperation.

'Oh, God! If I reach home safe, I shall sell my palace and offer the proceeds to the needy!'

After a while, to everyone's astonishment, the storm abated and all was calm. The ship now floated on smooth sea and reached the harbour safely.

Now the rich man regretted his hasty offer to God. 'Why was I in such a stupid haste? Now, how can I escape from the promise of offering?' he pondered.

Once back in his hometown, the rich man announced that he was going to sell his palace. Most of the rich people thronged to buy it, competing with one another.

He addressed a large gathering and declared the price of his palace as just $ 1.

All those who gathered, were stunned. 'Had the sea voyage turned him mad?' they wondered in confusion. And the rich man had something more to add...

'I will sell my palace only to a person who is willing to buy my cat! – only then my palace is available for $1. But, the cat has a price.' People thought what a deal – Palace for $1 and a cat with it. Why not?

'What is price of the cat?', a bidder asked.

'$ 1 million!'

The buyers were now totally bemused. However, as the palace was worth more than a million dollars, one of bidders bought the cat for $ 1 million and the palace for $ 1.

The rich man declared 'Lord, now as I promised, I donate $ 1 from the sale proceeds of my palace to the poor. Since the cat is mine, I keep $ 1 million... So my promise is kept.'

We are so manipulative that we ourselves are not aware of our manipulation. This is the height of manipulation.

Does God ask us for this and that? We are the ones who offer all kinds of things to Him in the name of prayer and vows. We pester Him constantly, saying 'I shall give you this and you give me that!' as if we are trading with him.

Some even stoop so low to bargain with God, 'If you get me $ 2 million, I shall donate $ 20,000 to your temple', as though offering Him a commission.

One cannot call it a 'prayer' when one gets entangled into vows and rituals without fully understanding their meaning. Prayer means fully understanding ourselves with sacredness.

The words of Jesus Christ may provide us with some clarity at this point.

'I was hungry, you offered food; I was thirsty, you offered water; I was sick, you offered help; I was in prison, you visited me; I was unclad, you gave me clothing. So, today I say unto you, whatever you do unto the least of your brethren, you do that for me!'

Reflections

Yoga of Wisdom
Prayer is not a Demand Note.

Yoga of Action
The Divine honours no drafts where there are no deposits. Let there be a deposits of Gratitude in your Prayer.

THE POWER
THAT MOVES US!

What is anger? When do you get angry?

Stop for two minutes, take a piece of paper and write the answer to these questions!

I used to ask the same question wherever I went to conduct the 'LIFE' programme. Let me give you some of the answers that I get.

'I get angry, when children do not obey me.

I get angry, when scolded in public.

I get angry, when my colleague blunders.

I get angry, when spoken of, behind my back'

The list is endless. Let us stop here and focus at anger and understand what it is.

When we deem ourselves to be inferior, there is a reaction and it shows up as anger.

When a person calls us 'donkey', we retaliate by calling him 'monkey.' This is reaction.

When we react, external situations control us. In the management lexicon the word used more often is pro-active, not reactive.

What is the difference between these two words?

The following Zen story throws more light on this.

There was a Samurai. After winning a war, he was returning home with his army. On the way, he passed through a forest. In the forest, a monk was deep in meditation. The Samurai bowed and asked humbly, 'Oh! Monk! Which is the way to heaven and which is the way to hell?'

The monk did not respond. Now the Samurai repeated his question a little more loudly. The monk still did not respond. The third time, the Samurai roared the question in a thunderous voice that shook the very tree under which the monk was meditating. Now the monk opened his eyes and said sternly,

'You stupid fellow! Why did you disturb my meditation?'

Now the Samurai was really furious. He immediately pulled out his sword and raised it to kill the monk. The monk said with a smile, 'This is the way to hell!'

The Samurai realised his folly. The truth dawned on him and his anger abated. 'The monk called me 'stupid' not to chide me but to teach me the truth...' He gently placed his sword in the sheath. And the monk said, 'This is the way to heaven!'

When the monk rebuked the Samurai in front of his soldiers, he was angry. 'How could this monk rebuke me in front of my soldiers!, I have been demeaned; the respect for me is gone! Now how will these fellows show me any regard in the future?' ran his thoughts, lowering his self-esteem, filling him with regret and sorrow. So, he failed to think and hence, drew out his sword - this is 'reaction.' To react - is the gate to hell.

'The reason to call the Samurai stupid was not to belittle him; but to answer his question in an indirect way. The Samurai was quick to grasp the teaching of the monk. Soon the sword found its place in the sheath - this is 'pro-action.' To respond – is the gate to heaven.

Hell and Heaven are the states-of-mind.

When we get angry with others, we lose our balance, our blood pressure rises and limbs tremble. By being angry, irrespective of the situation around us, punishment is meted out to us in the form of anger. We are responsible for our state.

Reflections

Yoga of Wisdom
Reactive Mind is Hell;
Responsive Mind is Heaven

Yoga of Action
The Ability to Respond is Responsibility

THINK BEFORE YOU MARRY!

A magnanimous person comes to a mental hospital to celebrate his birthday. He distributes sweets among the inmates.

He sees a patient hanging from a ceiling fan and screaming, 'Laila, Laila!'

On inquiry, the staff tell him, 'Well, it is nothing new! He was deeply in love with a girl. She left him and married someone else. Thus, he has become mad!'

He moves on and goes to another side of the hospital...he spots yet another patient hanging from the ceiling fan upside-down, shouting, 'Laila, Laila!'

'Who is this?' asks the visitor. 'He is the one who married that Laila!' answers the staff!

This is of course a joke...but it is well worth looking into the reasons why the love life and married life of many remain highly unsatisfactory these days.

Particularly, married life!

There is a basic reason for this state. It is because we think that marriage would bring us joy! What a wrong assumption!

129

The lamp is not light. Buildings are not home. Books are not knowledge. Looking at medicine, disease will not get cured.

Only when one lives lovingly in a house, it becomes a home. Only when books are read, they provide knowledge. Only by taking the medicine, one gets cured.

So is it with married life. Happiness does not come from marrying a like-minded boy or girl and being together forever.

If a husband and wife walk in different paths with diverse desires, then married life would not be successful. What is important is how they utilize each other's strengths for the success of their married life.

But those who marry with the idea that marriage and joy are one and the same, look for joy in marriage. When they fail to find joy, they feel disappointed! Marriage is also like a lamp. Only when the husband and wife light it together, it would bring illumination …. that is joy!

Recently, a young man came to me and said, 'Swamiji, I love a girl and want to marry her. She is beautiful. She is also well educated. Her father is rich enough. If I marry her, I will be happy!'

He had brought his girl friend along and she was waiting in the aisle. I asked him to bring her along.

'Why are you planning to marry him?', I asked the girl.

'My lover is highly cultured. He has good qualities and is very humorous. He is hardworking and sure to come up in life. So, he can keep me happy!' was her response.

Anyone viewing this couple superficially, would immediately declare, 'They are made for each other'! But I had my doubts. If they get married with their respective attitudes, they might not be happy.

Now I share with you a few thoughts that I expressed to them.

The man begs happiness from his girl friend, while the girl expects happiness from her boyfriend. When they get married to each other, what would be the result? How can one beggar running after happiness provide happiness to another beggar? Only beggary would increase.

My advice to married people is - do not think of how your partner makes you happy...instead, think how you make your partner happy!

Marriage works when we are givers of happiness and not beggars of happiness.

Take enticing items for an example. We are happy to receive them as gifts for ourselves. But isn't it much more joyous to offer gifts to others.. that too, to one's beloved?

'Giving' opens up a higher centre; hence joyous feeling arises.

Reflections

Yoga of Wisdom
If both beg for happiness, only beggary
increases.... in a marriage

Yoga of Action
Marriage is a commitment to change
each other's habits for better living.

THIRST...

(T)he major trouble in married life occurs when couples begin with a firm resolve that they should have no difference of opinion whatsoever!

How could a husband and wife born and brought up in different circumstances have the same opinion with respect to multiple issues in the family such as how to spend a holiday, what to purchase with the bonus amount....?

Sometimes there can be arguments between husband and wife. At such moments, one of them should be alert and manage the situation lest the discussion end up in a quarrel. In order to lower the tension, one of them should have a good sense of humour. But often, some people indulge in misplaced humour for the sake of being humorous. ....like this!

 Husband: I got trapped into marriage.

Wife: (in anger) You were after me; I was not after you. You used to follow me to the bus stop, office, home, everywhere!

Husband: (mockingly) True! The mouse-trap never runs after the mouse! It is the mouse that runs into the trap!

One can be sure that a flare-up would ensue between the two!

Another reason for upsets between husband and wife is 'comparison.'

'My sister is five years younger than I! She has bought non-stick cookware, vacuum cleaner! But being married to you, what have I got?' There are many wives who lament like this.

Now the husband's response to this is also another lament 'Look how sweet and cheerful your sister is with her husband! You are such a grumbler!'

Let me relate a story from Zen.

A crowd came flocking to see a Zen Monk from morning till night. Many would prostrate at his feet and worship him.

This became intolerable to the Commander of the army. So one day he went to the monk and asked, 'I am the Samurai of this country. I have thousands of soldiers under my command. But you, who are almost like a beggar, looking to someone else for your next meal, get more respect and regard than I do! How is that? I feel bad and jealous looking at you.'

The monk led him out of his hermitage. It was a full moon day. He pointed to the moon and asked, 'What is that?' The Samurai assertively said,' Moon.'

The monk then pointed out to the rose that was blooming in the garden and said, 'Now, what is this?' and the Samurai said, 'A Rose!'

'Does this Rose ever compare itself to the Moon and say, 'Oh, I am not white and bright like you? Does the Moon look at the rose and say, 'Why am I not colourful like you?'

The rose possesses one kind of beauty, while the moon is pretty and pleasant in another way.'

Even before the monk stopped speaking, the Samurai realized the truth. With moist eyes, he begged pardon of the monk and left in peace. He realised each one of us is unique in one's own way. Let us rejoice in our uniqueness.

There is yet another story to show how far comparisons can upset some people.

A dog, having lost its way, enters into a forest. It is a scorching sunny day and the heat is intolerable. Not able to find water, the dog wanders all around. Surprisingly it finds a pond full of water. Tired and thirsty, the dog rushes towards the water. As it bends down to drink, it sees its reflection in the pool. Now, its thirst is forgotten and it barks furiously at its own reflection. It becomes very weak and feeble. Just then a wind blows, ruffling the surface of the water, and the reflection disappears in the ripples. Now the dog eagerly drinks the water, as it is able to see the water and not its reflection!

Who prevented the dog from quenching its thirst? The dog itself.

We create our own obstacles by unwisely comparing ourselves to others.

Comparing ourselves to a neighbour's possessions or a relative's new acquisition, blinds many of us from seeing wonderful happenings in our own lives.

Reflections

Yoga of Wisdom
Egotism is the stumbling block in the Head.
The bigger the Heart, smaller the Head

Yoga of Action
Mental dieting of Egoistic 'I',
awakens the Divine 'Eye'

Contemplation

Don't worry about the future. Between the bomb and the terrorist there may not be any future.

We are so manipulative that we ourselves are not aware of our manipulations.

Which is the way to heaven and which one to hell?

Today is the tomorrow that you worried about yesterday.

Marriage is the coffin of love.

Let us rejoice in our uniqueness.

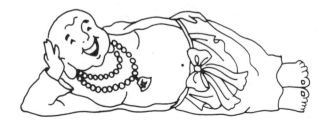

THIS MOMENT ...
THIS MINUTE .....
IS ABSOLUTE

W hich is the inseparable wealth in our lives?

I normally ask this question in my 'LIFE Program.'

Each one answers differently. But I say, '...this Minute...this Moment...is real.' No one can snatch it away from us. But many do not experience 'this moment...this passing moment...' fully. This is the hard fact that we have to face. Very often, we worry of the past or are lost in the anxiety of the future.

While at home, we worry about the workplace. While eating, our thoughts are not on the food. While bathing we do not wonder about the fabulous body – a gift given by God! We do not feel joyous that we are living today without a crisis! Our thoughts are like birds, flying everywhere. Just consider what would be the outcome!

As we drive, with our thoughts wandering elsewhere, we may meet with an accident. Similarly, accidents of various kinds would happen in our lives because of aimless thinking. I am not saying one should completely forsake thoughts about the past. Nor does it mean that one should make no plans for the future. I am only saying that just as we relish each drop of a cup of steaming hot coffee, we should savour each passing moment that makes up our life.

There would not be much difference between the first sip and the second sip of coffee. But, one moment in life is not the same as the next. Each moment is different.

In Zen Buddhism, there is a saying that one cannot bathe in the same river twice. That is to say, the water that is flowing in the river moves to another place, moment to moment. Similarly, life is in a state of constant change, moment to moment.

It does not suffice to have mere education, knowledge and ability...one must also have the awareness necessary for the present moment. If one does not possess that awareness, no matter what abilities and skills he possesses, these would be of no use to him. That is the reason behind the many tests that are conducted by big companies to verify whether applicants have presence of mind.

There was an expert musician. If he played violin, it would even rain in the desert. Once he had been to a circus. In the performance, a bear was dancing to the tune played by the violinist of the circus. This musician approached him and said, 'You can make only a trained bear to dance to your tune. But my music can make any animal dance!'

The circus violinist rejected this claim as sheer nonsense. An argument ensued, resulting in a duel.

The circus artist sent a lion in front of the musician. The lion, on hearing his music, began to gyrate in an ecstatic dance. Next, a cheetah was sent and that too began to dance. The circus artist sent a tiger...the musician continued to play nonchalantly. But the tiger was not enchanted by his music. On the contrary it charged at the musician, thirsty for his blood. The audience scattered in terror. The musician threw his violin in the air and ran for his life. Luckily, he somehow managed to escape from the tiger.

The trainers soon caught the tiger and locked it up in a cage. The exhausted musician accepted his defeat to the circus artist. However, he was still astounded as to why his music failed to charm that particular tiger. The circus artist explained with a smile, 'The reason is very simple. That tiger is stone deaf. By birth, it has this defect...it does not have ears or even the apertures for hearing. The audience soon noticed this and tried to escape. But you were so involved in your playing that you failed to notice this simple fact!'

All the wonderful skills the musician possessed were nullified due to lack of presence of mind.

Reflections

Yoga of Wisdom

Be alive to the present and stay clear.

Yoga of Action

No one climbed a mountain just by gazing at it. Act from the present.

CALCULATING MISERY!

Male or female, young or old; there is a great power within each one of us.

Earth has many seasons like summer, fall, spring and rain which the Sun does not have. Similarly, it is the body that goes through changes of aging from child to youth... to adulthood ....to old age while mind is ageless. We can keep our minds in total alertness and joy, at all ages!

'This is easier said than done,' you may think! Is it really possible?

Yes, it is one hundred per cent possible! But we need to practise certain things to achieve this. We need to see a lot, listen a lot!

'Swamiji, what are you saying? Every one has eyes and ears. Every one sees and listens! But is everyone full of vigour and joy?' you may well enquire.

Think for a while! Every one has pens and pencils. But does everyone become a writer or an artist? Just as pen and pencil are mere tools, so are eyes and ears. If only one knows how to use a pen and pencil does one become a writer or an artist? In the same way, if eyes and ears are used effectively, happiness can be attained!

Most of us focus our attention on what is not in front of us. We miss seeing things in front us.

A rich Italian father was celebrating his only son's birthday. The highlight of the day's programme was a football match.

The stadium was flooded with people who longed to watch the enthralling match between two famous teams of Italy. The crowd roared with joy as the teams competed with each other, but the birthday boy watched the game without enthusiasm. He looked at his father and said sulkily, 'Dad! Why are you so stingy!'

The father who had spent millions of dollars for the celebration for his only son's birthday, was perplexed. He looked at his son surprisingly.

The son explained, 'In this hot sun, look how these fellows are chasing only one ball. How sad? Could you not be little more generous in providing each one of them a ball so that they could play with them happily!'

At times, we are just like this boy! We fail to notice the joyful, energizing aspects of many incidents taking place in front of us. Instead, we brood on meaningless issues and miss all the fun in life.

Recently, a young man visited me at my Ashram in Bangalore. He was complaining for hours, 'My parents have done great injustice to me. My whole life is miserable due to this.'

This is what had happened...when he was a small boy, his parents did not send him to an English medium school due to which, he was unable to speak fluent English. According to him, this one aspect made him feel inferior to others.

After conversing with him for about an hour, I learnt certain facts about him. He had joined the same organisation where his father had worked and retired. The present job held by him was made available to him on the basis of 'job allotment to the heirs of ex-employees.'

Also, his parents had provided him a decent house in an extremely good locality, got him married to a girl of his choice. He even had access to many good things in life due to his parent's benevolence. In spite of all these he cribbed that life was unfair to him.

There are many such persons in this world. Instead of enjoying what they have, they magnify what they do not have and suffer thinking about what is not available.

It is the habit of some, to scrutinise expenses, pie to pie when they are on a tour with their family. They neither cherish beautiful surroundings nor the company of their own kith and kin. The joy of being together is spoiled by the arithmetic; thus converting a joyous occasion into utter misery.

Reflections

Yoga of Wisdom

People are as happy as they decide to be.

Yoga of Action

Humanity's favourite sport is search for happiness. Search it wisely.

VISION THROUGH
A KEY HOLE

(T)his is a story about Mullah Nasruddin from Sufi literature.

Mullah returns home from work and his wife finds a long, black hair on his coat. Hell breaks loose!

'You are having an affair with a young girl!' she screams at Mullah. Patiently he tries to explain, 'Look, I walked through a crowded market place. Somehow this hair has clung to my coat...believe me!'

She refuses to believe him and continues to rave and rant. The next day, when Mullah returns home from work, she notices a grey hair on his coat.

'Alas! Yesterday it was a young girl, and today it is an old woman! You womanizer!! Now my whole life is ruined!' she screams, rolling on the ground in tears.

The day after that, while returning home, Mullah remembered his wife's antics and carefully dusts his coat before entering the house. She hurriedly checks his clothes but finds no hair. Mullah is about to heave a sigh of relief...but no, it is not to be! His wife shouts in anger, -

147

'What a scoundrel you are! Today you had an affair with a bald woman?' and begins to wail more fiercely than on the previous days!

This misery is the result of our mind not seeing the beauty in front of us but instead, wandering in imagination and seeing things that are not in front of us.

Even in listening, many of us fail to grasp important points, or listen erroneously. The result is nothing but unnecessary tension.

Jack and James were close friends. They also worked in the same office. Once, Jack faced a financial crisis at home. In anger, he had flung his wallet at his wife and come to the office. At the workplace too, he was tense. He picked quarrels with every one in the office. His language was rude and insulting. Noticing this, James took him out for lunch. Jack hesitated since he had no money, but James pacified him, offering to pay for the food. Jack was hungry since morning; he ordered for many food items and began to eat. At the same time, he felt uncomfortable eating at his friend's cost.

At this juncture, James, with an intention to advise Jack on his rude behaviour at the office, said, 'Jack, you have to control your tongue!'

Jack misunderstood his advice and became angry. He thought that James was referring to his eating by using James's money. Oblivious that they were at the restaurant, he grabbed James by his shirt and snarled,

'How can you behave in such a mean manner?'

Now it was James's turn to lose his temper. Soon a fist fight ensued. In the process, crockery was broken. Jack fell on the splinters and injured himself. The restaurant staff intervened and stopped the fight. Jack was taken to a hospital for treatment and James returned to the office.

However, James was unable to concentrate on his work. He was full of remorse for his bad behaviour and chided himself for momentarily losing patience at the restaurant. So he immediately visited the hospital to see Jack.

When Jack saw James entering the hospital, his blood began to boil, as he was still seething in anger. He concluded that James had come to continue the fight which was left midway at the restaurant. He was unable to see his friend's good intention. James asked out of compassion, 'How do you feel now?'

Taking this to be the height of sarcasm, Jack flared up once again and raised his hand on James.

More important than the mere words, we need to understand the context in which they are spoken. This is the truth that can be gathered from the above narrative.

Unable to understand such simple matters, many amongst us, heap trouble on ourselves.

Seeing and hearing...these two activities are not done by our eyes and ears only. At times, we view the world through our perception. Our perceptions in turn are guided by the preconceived notions we form of persons and things. Through this keyhole called perception, we view the vast world around us. Most of these perceptions are foggy and baseless. Hence, our eyes and ears focus on the unreal.

Reflect on these examples:

Doctor : Old age is the cause for your hand pain

Patient :   Don't think I am stupid. The other hand is just as old and I have no pain.

***

Albert : How much did you sell your car for?

Joseph : '$ 20000'

Albert : 'You got a good price!'

Joseph : 'But, if I knew that rascal was not going to pay me, I would have charged him thrice as much.'

Reflections

Yoga of Wisdom
*Perceiver pollutes the perception and one perceives
the perceived as an extension of the perceiver.*

Yoga of Action
*Renounce the distorted perceiver and
rejoice the perceived*

Contemplation

Treat problems as challenges and have fun with life.

Some complain that the stepping stone to success hurt and injure their feet.

Many people have faith in their doubts and doubt their faith.

An enlightened man is never confused by what he can't understand, but a fool is sure to be.

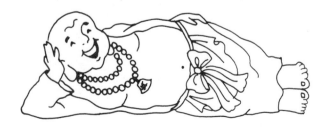

WHO IS THE CULPRIT?

The ability to see is a great gift. But we do not see with our eyes fully open. A few of us use the eyes for sleep more often than for sight. There are yet others who just stay afloat in a dreamland with eyes wide open; without seeing the objects in front of them!

We are awake ...We are not sleeping nor dreaming ... Can we be sure that we are able to see things as they really are?

Many are not even able to see that. We normally wear coloured glasses through which we see the world. By coloured glasses I refer to the perceptions of any person. Perceptions are the opinions we form without any basis......on our relatives, friends, neighbours, acquaintances, things........

Management work-shops use certain puzzles to open people to their perceptions. Let me give you a simple example from one of them.

According to Roman numerals, the number nine is written as IX. Now the challenge is, by using just a single line, we must convert nine into six.

153

Now, before reading on, pause for two minutes and attempt doing it. Just by using a single line, change nine into six. Why don't you try?

Here is the answer - Roman 'IX', is 9 in Arabic numerals. Now consider the Roman numeral digits as English alphabets... can you see alphabets 'I' and 'X'? Now simply add the letter 'S' before them. Aha! Now 'NINE' has become 'SIX'!

When I said single line, normally the 'mindset' in most of us, would conceive a straight line. Why? The Alphabet 'S' is actually a single line... a curved line! But not many of us think so. It is only our perception that prevents us from finding a solution to the puzzle.

Similarly, our perception could be a block, preventing us from seeing the truth.

Listen to this story...

It was a dense forest, full of wild beasts. A woodcutter lived in the forest with his beautiful wife. The woodcutter used to drink liquor and beat his wife. This agony continued for several days. The wife was soon fed up with the routine. She used to load logs into a boat, take it across the river, sell it and use the money for buying provisions. This was her daily routine. As time went by, she became friendly with the owner of the provision shop across the river.

On a new Moon day...it was pitch dark. The woodcutter was drunk to his teeth and began to torture her cruelly. Thoroughly tired of his behaviour, she came out of the hut in the middle of the dark night. A thought flashed in her mind...why not go to the provision shop owner? That would definitely be better than this misery!

Now she needed the boat to cross over to the other side of the river. She woke up the boatman; but he refused to ferry her across the river. Suddenly, she remembered a small wooden bridge across the river, about two miles away. She also remembered vaguely that a cheetah used to be habitually seen around the bridge, but she was in no mood to pay any heed to that warning. All that she wanted was to get away. So she walked towards the wooden bridge.

The next morning, her mutilated body was found near the bridge. The cheetah had attacked her during the night.

Now, read out this story to your family members. In the end, ask them individually, 'Who was responsible for the death of the woodcutter's wife?'

One would say, 'It was the woodcutter, the cursed drunkard!'

Another would blame the woman saying that she was immoral and so sought her own gory end because of her bad thinking.

Yet another would say, 'it is the boatman who was merciless and allowed her to walk alone...so he is at fault.'

Someone may even venture to say that it was the provision shop owner who enticed her into adultery.

The question is one and the same, yet there are so many responses. Why? It comes from the perception of each individual. Each one has his or her own perception.

In the night, as you look up at the lofty peepul tree, you may only see its branches and its rustling leaves. Only when you peer through them, you would notice the brightness of the Moon hidden behind them. In the same way, at first, when you look at something or someone, your perception would cover your view and hide the truth.

Without going by the first impressions, stop; look again without likes and dislikes; look with a clear and unbiased mind at the same thing, taking time to assimilate facts, and you will then see the reality...the truth.

Reflections

Yoga of Wisdom
Don't be a Victim of your point of view

Yoga of Action
Understand that there are many variables;
Reward yourself for the right action
that flows.

Contemplation

Each one has his or her own perception.

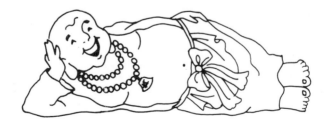

GOD IS IN OUR HEARTS - WHY?

One fine day, God wished to enjoy his creation and descended on the earth.

Those devotees, who recognised Him, clamoured around Him like beggars and pestered Him for favours. 'Please give me lots of jewels! Please give me plenty of money!' They chased Him with requests.

God ran from place to place in order to escape this nuisance... He went to villages, towns, cities but nowhere could He escape from the people's nagging. He found their pleas unbearable. So, he ran towards a temple; there too beggars were in queue with bowls in their hands! He was utterly perplexed as to what to do. Finally, He struck upon an idea.

'Man does not seek within... nor does introspect about himself! No one delves into one's own heart! So, that is the best place to hide from this maddening crowd. No one will be able to see me!' With such a thought, God entered into the heart of mankind and hid there!

This is a very comical reply to a very serious question as to why God resides within our hearts!

Most of us constantly think as to what we can get from others. Hence, we rarely contemplate on what we can give to others. Perchance, should we provide a lighting fixture to a temple, we paint our name on the tube so large that no light can ever emanate from that tube!

According to Hindu dharma, when something is donated, it is deemed, 'This is not mine any more!' In Sanskrit, *'na mama'* means, 'Not mine.' By declaring 'it is not mine' while donating and still painting the donor's name over it, means what? What dharma does it conform to?

Just consider for a moment. From the time we wake up; the paste, the brush that we use .... until we go to bed at night, using a mosquito repellent ..... all the multifarious things that we use throughout the day...are made and provided by hundreds of other people, for us!

It is enough if we think for a moment, 'I have received so many things from this society in which I live. In return, what have I done for the society?' We would realize how deeply we are indebted to the world around us.

God has given us a wonderful life. Not all the brilliant scientists with their combined effort can make bodies such as ours. From the food that we partake daily, to this globe that rotates relentlessly, the wonders within and without ..... the gifts provided to us are unlimited. Do we express our gratitude for the benevolence?

The very first teaching in the Veda is 'Learn to be grateful.' The Sanskrit word 'Stuti' means 'praise unto HIM' and one must utter His word in total gratitude.

When we reckon all the words that we use in our daily conversation, the one most often used would be 'Thanks!' We have to ask, 'Does this come from our heart or lips?'

There was a technical snag encountered on a plane in mid-air. The plane began to wobble and the airhostess announced, 'There is a small problem in the engine. The pilot is attending to it and soon it would be set right.'

But as time went on, it was obvious that the problem had aggravated and the plane was flying haphazardly. The airhostess announced, 'My dear passengers! Inspite of the best efforts put in by the pilot, we are unable to rectify the problem. We are sorry, the plane may explode in a few minutes. We however thank you for flying with our airlines!'

Leaving the passengers to fend for themselves, she fixed her parachute and jumped off the plane!

So is our 'Thanks' to others; many a time, a mere formality like the words of the airhostess!

Reflections

Yoga of Wisdom
Existence gives us the necessary ingredients for our daily bread, but expects us to do the baking.

Yoga of Action
To know and not act on what you know is equal to not knowing.

SWAMIJI, WHY DO YOU SAY 'THANK YOU'?

How to express gratitude?

The word 'thanks' should not be uttered mechanically. It is something expressed from one's heart to another. When someone expresses gratitude from the depth of his heart, his hands would move together in obeisance..the lips would tremble...tears would well up in his eyes!

This is a story from Zen Buddhism.

He was the owner of a small restaurant. From morning to night, he would toil in his restaurant. Yet, his heart was centred in spiritual thoughts. His only wish was to meet at least one Zen monk in his lifetime, but his workload did not permit him to go in search of a monk. Every one, including his staff as well as his regular customers knew of his desire.

It was not the habit of the Zen monks to wear the normal garb of monks ... saffron robes or any special attire meant for those who had renounced worldly life. They normally dressed like any of the other ordinary Japanese citizens. So it was very difficult to identify a monk.

One particular day, the restaurant owner was very busy. Busy as he was, it was however his habit to observe all his customers. He noticed two men were drinking tea seated in a corner table. As he watched them, his joy knew no bounds!

'The Zen monks, who I waited for all these years, have come to my restaurant at last!' he exclaimed happily.

The two men, in fact, were Zen monks. Seeing his exuberance, they accepted him as their disciple. He made his son take charge of the restaurant and was about to follow the monks. One of his customers then asked him, 'How did you find out these two were Zen monks?'

'I found out from the way they were seated, the way they held the tea cups in reverence, the way they sipped the tea with gratitude ..... every moment was filled with love. They were radiating serenity all around', he replied as he walked away with them.

He himself later became a Zen monk. Not only that, he also established a novel method of meditation known as 'Zen Tea Meditation' in memory of those two monks who led him to enlightenment.

What is this 'Zen Tea Meditation'?

Yes, you guessed it right! It is nothing but drinking a cup of tea with a great sense of prayer & gratitude. Even today, in Japan, 'Zen Tea Ceremony' takes place. In this ceremony, the Japanese hold cups of tea in both their hands, and sip it with a deep relish, love and gratitude.

God has showered benevolence on the Japanese in many ways, as their attitude in expressing gratitude, is unmatched.

But many of us may ask, 'What has HE given us except poverty and hunger? Why should we be grateful to God?'

In Islam, there is a sect known as Sufi. A Sufi monk and his disciples were wandering in the forest. It was scorching under the sun. Thorns hurt them as they walked bare foot. Unmindful of these sufferings, the monk walked on and on. There were no houses in sight to beg for alms, nor any waterways to quench his thirst on the way! Soon it was night. The monk and his disciples got ready to sleep, without having eaten or drunk anything during the whole day.

The monk prayed aloud, 'Oh, God! Thank you for all that you gave me today!'

This really irked his disciples who were dying of hunger and thirst. Controlling their anger, they asked, 'God did not give us anything. Yet you are thanking Him. So what is the meaning of your prayer?'

The Sufi monk replied with a smile, 'Who told you that God did not give us anything? Just as a mother knows what to give and what not to give to her child, God knows well what to give and what not to give us. Today, He has given us hunger; an opportunity to fast. Whatever He does, He does it rightly. Therefore, I thanked Him.'

Reflections

Yoga of Wisdom

Discover the power of gratitude and existence will comfort you.

Yoga of Action

Value the power of gratitude. Let it be your mantra or inner song. Then you will grow and not just swell.

EXPERIENCE OF TWO KINDS!

𝕿his was during the war between the US and Vietnam.

The war had devastated Vietnam. People lost their homes, children lost their parents, and wives lost their husbands...... the country was flooded with blood and tears.

To assess the outcome of the war, the American government had deployed two commanders to Vietnam.

Looking at the terrifying scenes on the aftermath of war; mutilated soldiers fighting for their lives, mothers grieving by the side of dead babies ......the sight was unbearable for one commander. He ended his life by committing suicide.

The other commander also witnessed a similar scenario. On seeing them, however, all his troubles back home seemed too minor to worry about. After returning to his country, he spoke to his countrymen about the problems encountered by the Vietnamese. His native people, who were filled with trifles such as 'Money that I have lent has not been returned...I am unable to buy my next car' ......' were highly impressed and touched by his narration. Soon, he was invited all over the country to narrate his experiences! He became a very rich man, merely by narrating his Vietnam experience!

Now, one commander commits suicide! The other overcoming his own trouble and helps others to tide over their troubles! The crux of the matter is, both of them saw similar war strife scenario; but their perceptions were different.

Let me tell you another example before I come to the point.

There was a multi-national company making shoes. In order to assess the level of demand for their shoes, the Director of the company deputed a manager to a country in Africa. The manager cut short his tour with a report 'We cannot sell any shoes in that country!' When asked for an explanation, he said, 'People walk bare footed; No one wears shoes there. Hence no potential.'

The Director was not a man to accept 'No' for an answer. So he sent another man to study the situation. On his return, jumping with joy, he declared, 'There is a huge market for our shoes in that country!'

'How is that?' asked the Director.

'People walk bare footed; no one wears shoes in the whole country! Hence, huge potential for our product' was the reply.

This is what we have to learn from the above story. Every person's experience is different in situations like work, trade, home..... But as far I can see, all experiences can be categorized into two types – good and bad. Whatever the experience, if a lesson can be learnt from it, it is a good one! If one cannot learn or has not learnt a lesson from it, it is a bad one!

> Thomas Alva Edison, who invented the electric bulb, did not succeed in his very first attempt. He invented it only after almost one thousand failures. Someone once asked him, 'You made one thousand experiments. Out of them, 999 failed and only one succeeded. Isn't it so?'
>
> For that, his reply was, 'How can you say that I did not find out anything during 999 experiments? To invent one working bulb, I learnt how not to make 999 non-working ones!'

In every situation, see a possibility; like the manager saw the possibility of selling shoes in a place where people were not wearing shoes.

Reflections

Yoga of Wisdom
Failure is a fertilizer for success.

Yoga of Action
Learn from failure. Failure in life is one who lives and fails to learn.

NIAGARA SYNDROME!

Whenever I am on tour during exam time, whether it is Bombay, Bangalore, or Hyderabad, the students ask me, 'Swamiji I am unable to study with full concentration. Friends distract my attention from studies to topics like cricket, movies, etc.. How can I solve this problem?'

Recently in Madras, I met a student who asked me the same question.

'What are you studying?' I asked.

'I am doing Chartered Accountancy'

'That means, you must have been under one auditor for about three years in training?' I asked.

'Yes! Now my training period is over. I have taken up accounting work in a firm. Evenings are spent being with friends and watching TV. Even if I consider studying during nights, I feel like reading sports magazines ...., just to lighten up my tiredness of working throughout the day; in the process I am not able to study for exams.'

Look at his value system! He gives great importance to his job during the day, sitting in an air-conditioned room with top executives! He values the earnings received at work.

Next, his value system is being with friends, watching TV and cricket matches. No one can say 'this is right' or 'this is wrong.' If he had aimed that passing in the exam was most important, then he would give more importance to his studies than his friends and TV. I told him this, but he did not accept it.

'I give great importance to study. Getting a CA degree is really important to me. TV is not important to me. But once I see the programmes, I am drawn to the TV and I immediately forget my studies,' he said.

'It is because you give importance to TV, you have an interest in it. It is only your thoughts that decide your actions. If CA is important, you must re-evaluate your value system; you must try to change it!' I said.

After two days, he came again.

'Swamiji! I tried to change my value system. But it is not that easy!' he said.

'All right! Now, between TV, friends and passing CA exam, write the pros and cons of your decision on a piece of paper. In case you are able to relegate TV, friends to a secondary status, then too, jot down all the pros and cons and see what you get! Then you would easily understand what is important in your life.' I said.

The possibility of changing his value system by writing down the pros and cons brightened his eyes. I could see fresh hope dawning on him.

You have to plan today for your future happiness! Otherwise, sorrow and misery will encompass your tomorrows.

If you are going to rationalise that you cannot really plan your life and simply take life as it comes, you too would become like the protagonist of the following story!

A man was travelling in a boat. Cool waters, dense trees swaying overhead along the banks of the river on either side, the twittering of the birds, gently wafting breeze, all this enchanted him and he was absorbed in the beauty of the place. He allowed the boat to float of its own accord, along with the flow of the river. He never even glanced at the direction in which the boat was going. As the boat was floating effortlessly, he did not have to use the oars. It was very comfortable for him to travel in the boat without expending any energy and he was very happy.

After a while, the wind rose and the boat began to move faster. The lazy fellow was now overjoyed!

'Oh, wow! My journey is now really fast!' he roared in pleasure. A little later, there was a distant roar, faintly audible. 'Great, now nature is playing an orchestra for me!'

Suddenly the boat began to flounder and started to capsize towards a waterfall. Only when the boat slid down the roaring waterfall, did he realize what was happening. The river on which he was travelling was thundering downwards from a vast height in the form of the Niagra waterfall!

Even as he tried in vain to control the boat with his oars, it was too late. There was no use for the oars. He could not prevent himself from falling down into the waterfall.

The lethargic mentality of this person is called 'Niagara Syndrome.'

If you don't plan, you will perish. Don't allow your life to come to the edge of the Niagra falls to make a decision to change; be it in health, relationship, family, business.... Don't be blown by your unintelligent logic. Here is an example:

 Friend : What is your age?

Mullah : I don't know.

Friend :Why?

Mullah : It is constantly changing, day by day.

Reflections

Yoga of Wisdom
Plan or Perish

Yoga of Action
Plan purposefully. Prepare prayerfully.
Proceed positively. Pursue persistently.

Contemplation

Fear not tomorrow. God, the Almighty is already there.

Be thankful if your work is a little harder than you want. A knife can't be sharpened on a piece of velvet.

Be grateful for what you have and not sad for what you don't have.

Be a possibility thinker.

If you don't plan, you will perish.

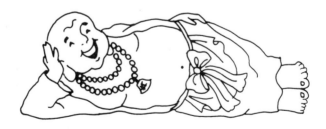

VISION 1...2...3...

A fisherman went to sell fish in a crowded market for the first time. He chose a place by the side of a compound. He put a board reading 'Fresh Fish Sold Here!' Standing back, he viewed his own handiwork, checked if everything was okay. He read what he wrote, once again.

Now, he doubted 'Would any one sell stale fish? Then why to use the word 'fresh'?' So, he erased the word 'fresh.'

The board read 'Fish Sold Here.' When he saw the signboard again, he wondered 'Have I brought the fish to donate? It is well understood that I am going to sell it...so he thought the word 'sold' is unnecessary.' He erased that word too.

Now the signboard showed 'Fish Here.' After seeing the signboard, he began to laugh. It was obvious that the fish was here and not somewhere else! So why the word 'Here'?' And he removed that word also.

Now all that remained on the signboard was the word 'Fish.' Finally, he saw the signboard and thought, 'anyone who comes to the market can identify by the very smell of fresh fish. As soon as they see the fish, they would recognize it! There was no doubt about that! Then why at all the word 'Fish'? So he erased the word 'Fish'! Now the signboard was bare and empty!

All our problems are like the signboard of the fisherman. Once we learn to view the problems in the right perspective, our problems too would disappear. But the saddest part here is, most of us do not even know how to view things!

The word for philosophy in Sanskrit literally means Vision (darshan). It means 'to see.' What are the things necessary for seeing? Is it sufficient to have eyes? 'No, eyes alone are not enough, one must have awareness', says Lord Krishna.

Only when we have awareness, shall we know to discern the difference between things, people and ourselves.

'How many houses do you own? What is the market value? Which car do you use?'

We ask such questions while we talk about things. Things must be viewed in a mathematical way. Things must be viewed as tools and used as tools!

Next, how do we see human beings? One cannot measure human beings with the same yardstick that we use to measure things. Affectionate father, loving mother, dear sister, and grateful friend... should be the yardstick; yardstick of love, affection and relationship.

But in reality, what do we do?

Things that are to be used as tools, are placed with an attachment that is akin to an emotional relationship! And persons who we should love - mother, father, brother, children, friends..... we use them as tools to fulfil our needs!

Things should be seen mathematically and persons should be seen with love. Right! How should we see ourselves within? In order to understand how we see ourselves, first we must understand what we do mean by 'WE.'

There are three dimensions to our bodies. First of all, the material body ... the one made up of flesh and bones. Second, the energy body .... the one made up of our knowledge, thoughts, mind.... The final one is known as 'Awareness' - in Sanskrit, it is known 'Sakshi.'

Can you see how we have come back to the starting point?

In order to face problems, what we need is 'Objective Vision'; and in order to see something, we need 'Awareness.'

It is wrong on our part to think that we should not have problems. The only place where there can be no problem is the graveyard. That is to say, only dead people do not have problems. All those who are alive would surely have problems. If there were no problems, then life itself would be dull.

Tripping , getting hurt, suffering with pain, chasing victory with pain, moment of glory being snatched away by some one ...... all these things happen not only in life but also in football. But for a football champion, every problem that he faces is an interesting challenge.

When a football player kicks the ball towards the goal, if the goalkeeper and the players of the opposite team remain idle, without offering any resistance, would that game become exciting? Would that game be interesting to players? Or would anyone be interested in watching such a game at all?

Just think for a moment...!

Learn to enjoy every problem in life. Let your ability to enjoy be above your problem. Create waves of joy wherever you go.

Reflections

Yoga of Wisdom
Treat problem as an opportunity to grow

Yoga of Action
Act with a commitment that every problem contains within itself the ingredients of solution.

Contemplation

Think of doubt as an invitation welcoming you to think.

Man loves objects and uses people instead of loving people and using objects.

Only dead people don't have problems.

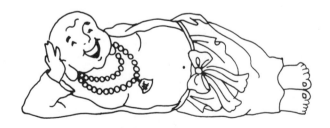

AN ORACLE...
AND A MIRACLE

𝕴 was talking about problems.

One is external, beyond our control; the other is internal, we inflict on ourselves by our own choice. The main cause for this is greed!

A Zen Monk visited a small village. The villagers gathered around him and placed their requests before him, 'Please help us get rid of our problems; let our desires be fulfilled', and said, 'only then would our lives be full of joy.'

The monk listened to them, silently. The next day, he arranged for a heavenly voice.....

'Tomorrow at mid-day a miracle is going to take place in this village. Pack all your problems in an imaginary sack, take it across the river and leave it there. Then, in the same imaginary sack, put everything that you want ... gold, jewellery, food ...., and bring it home! You do this and your desires would materialise.'

The villagers were in doubt as to whether this oracle was true or not. However the voice from the heaven astounded them. They thought they had nothing to lose by following the instruction. If it were true, then they would really get what they wanted and if it were false, any way, it wasn't a big deal! So they decided to do what was told.

Next day, at noon, they all packed their troubles in an imaginary sack and went across the river, left it there and brought back all that they thought would bring them happiness ... gold, car, house, jewellery, diamonds......!

On their return, they were really stunned! Whatever the oracle had said had come true! The man, who wanted a car, found one parked in front of his house. The one who wished for a palatial house, found that his house had turned into one. They were all so happy! Their joy knew no bounds!

But alas! The joy and celebration lasted for a while. Soon they began to compare themselves with their neighbours...each one felt the person next door was happier and richer than himself. Now they began to talk amongst themselves to pry out more details. The next moment, they were full of remorse.

'I had asked for a simple chain, while the girl next door had asked for an ornate gold necklace and got it! I just asked for a house but the man residing opposite asked for a mansion. We too should have asked for such things! It was a wonderful opportunity, the chance of a lifetime...we let it slip by, foolishly!'

Such were the thoughts that occupied their minds. Once again they returned to the monk and piled their complaints in front of him. The village was once again plunged into frustration and discontent.

Many feel that they cannot be happy if they have problems. I wish to tell them something more.

Do not link your happiness to problems. Problems are there in everybody's life. Tell yourself this 'Let problems be there on one side...I would still continue to be happy!' and remain cheerful. This does not mean that one should not think of resolving the problems.

Who could have faced more problems than Lord Krishna? Was not his uncle Kamsa plotting to kill him even before Lord Krishna's birth? In the war of Mahabharata, he served as the charioteer of Arjuna. Did Arjuna not create problems in the last minute by casting off his armour and declining to fight? In the battlefield of Kurukshetra, each day was fraught with problems of all kinds. Each arrow that was aimed at Arjuna said hello to Krishna. Despite this, the joyful smile ever adorned his face!

Lord Krishna has expounded further in Bhagavad Gita. 'Learn to view equally both sorrow and joy; be open to joy, be open to sorrow. They are the two sides of the same coin. Try to learn from both ... clarity will emerge. This clarity will bring you bliss!'

Reflections

Yoga of Wisdom
An untrained mind creates its own prison of unhappiness

Yoga of Action
Dis-identify with an unhappy mind and treasure your experiences.

DULL MOVIE...
DISLIKED SCENES...!

Recently I was in Hyderabad to conduct the 'LIFE Program.' For some of the participants, certain painful experiences of their past still remained as deep seated scars in their hearts – and they keep coming again and again to ruin the present moment.

'The painful memories often raise their ugly heads and depress us. How can we escape from them?' they asked.

Very often during 'LIFE Programs', participants would share their inner traumas. I would also encourage them to speak. I used to ask them, 'What is the injury that remains buried as a wound in your heart for a long time?'

One person said, 'My friend and I got together and started a civil contract business. Since I was in government service, I ran the firm in my friend's name. Very soon the business prospered. In order to concentrate on the work, I even resigned from my government job. Sometime later, for the purpose of filing income tax returns, I asked my friend for the account books of the company. And he said, 'Look, for the work that you are doing, take whatever pay you want. But don't come here asking about accounts and so on!' His words were like blistering barnacles to my ears.

187

'I had given him the responsibility of running the company, including signing powers, fully trusting him. Now I was helpless! This was the company I had started by investing all that I had, including the money got by selling the family jewels. I simply wiped the tears of frustration from my eyes and walked out. All those years of hard toil and sweat were snatched from me in a trice. This happened to me many years ago. Later I began another construction company, which is now yielding good profits. Yet, the treachery of my friend still makes me feel choked and tears well up in my eyes!'

Next a young woman came forward to speak. She said, 'I fell in love with a man and married him. But from the beginning, my mother-in-law looked down on me with hostility. Within a few weeks of our marriage, a great grief struck our house. My sister-in-law was widowed in an accident. My mother-in-law began cursing me as the cause for the accident. When my relatives came to express their condolences, she chided me in their presence saying, 'You are full of ill luck! The moment you stepped into the house, the tragedy took place. You don't have a place here, get out at once!'

On the same day, my husband and I left the house. After a few years, my younger brother-in-law got married. Though my husband was the eldest son of the family he was not invited for the wedding. Later on, my father-in-law turned seriously ill. We visited him. Despite being almost on his deathbed, his anger towards me had not waned.

My mother-in-law said, 'You are a demon who brings bad luck! Even if the air around you touches my husband, he would die! So, get out!' As soon as we returned home, to my bad luck, my father-in-law passed away and my husband who was his first-born child, did not even have the opportunity to see his face before he was cremated!

'Many years have since passed, and I have been living here in Hyderabad, several hundred kilometers away from the town where my mother-in-law resides. We are fairly comfortable, blessed with children and prosperity. Yet, every time I remember the insults that were heaped on me...,more on my husband, my heart aches at the injustice! What am I to do?'

Similarly, many poured out their past agonies and scars. I did not wish to answer their queries directly. Instead, I began like this 'Give me the name of a very boring movie, that you dislike!'

Each mentioned one movie or the other.

'All right! Now go, fetch the movie from a video parlour and watch it all through the night, again and again!'

'Oh, no! I cannot do that! I would die of boredom! Tell me something else that I can do!' they all pleaded.

'Well, the treachery of friends, torture of mother-in-law..... are also painful scenes that you dislike immensely! Why do you insist on playing them and replaying them over and over again on the mental screen? While you refuse to watch an imaginary film that you merely dislike and find boring, how can you replay those scenes that you loathe on your mental screen? Allow yourself to forget them...the wound would dry up and the scar would vanish by itself!' I said.

The reason why small children are always happy is because they do not carry burdens from the past...they forget painful incidents very quickly, but they bring up joyful memories again and again and enjoy them. We too should learn to be like children. That would considerably lessen the burden that we carry in our hearts.

To put all this in a nutshell, the past must only tutor us, not torture us!

In such a space, a hidden intelligence will surface which will guide us in a mysterious way.

Reflections

> ### *Yoga of Wisdom*
> *Transform your Mind and*
> *Transcend Unhappiness*
>
> ### *Yoga of Action*
> *Learn from the Past, Rejoice the Present,*
> *Plan for the Future.*

Contemplation

Very few people live. Most of us are committing suicide by unwisely desiring.

Hope for the best and accept the worst.

Joy is not the absence of problems.

There are certain flowers that will not yield their fragrance untill they are crushed.

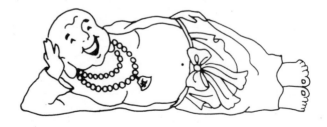

AN ARMOUR AROUND THE BODY

ⓣhere are several instances of joy and happiness in every one's life. Every time your heart feels heavy, please remind yourself of those happy moments, again and again. Then you would forget your hurt feelings and begin to float in the boat of happy memories. This technique is known as 'Super-imposing technique.'

Some may question as to how this is possible.

This is a story narrated by a lady hailing from a very prosperous family.

It was her birthday. When she woke up in the morning, she could scarcely believe her eyes. Her room was decorated with colourful balloons and glittering papers. During the previous night, her husband had taken trouble to decorate her room to celebrate her birthday. He had done the work noiselessly, with total care and love. When she learnt of this, she could not contain her joy. She hugged him to show her gratitude and affection.

Now, she came out of her room. Her parents who lived hundreds of miles away arrived on a surprise visit to give her a pleasant shock. Her only child presented her a gift.

All this made her as happy as she had never experienced before in her life!

She wore a new silk sari presented by her husband for the special occasion and went to a temple with the family. In the temple, her new silk sari got stained by the oil used for lighting the temple lamps that had spilt on the floor.

That's all...... the joy that she had experienced since that morning simply vanished. Her mind tormented by the oil stain that was dominating her thoughts so much that it shut out everything else. Later, to assuage her feelings, her husband took her out for dinner, then to a movie, bought her expensive gifts... She could however not forget the oil stain. The very thoughts of the oil stain tormented her throughout that eventful day!

When worrisome thoughts can be super-imposed on happy thoughts, is the reverse not possible? Yes, it is.

We have already mentioned about people who hurt others by their words. Just think for a moment about the type of people who get hurt by such words. Usually, only those with a low energy level would get easily affected by words and actions of others.

When a person's energy level is high, no one can hurt him!

Think of the moments in your life when you were at the peak of your energy levels. It may have been the day when you passed your final exam. Or the day you got a job! Or the day when your beloved accepted your love!

While your energy level was at its peak, no matter how sharp the words thrown at you are, they would not have bothered you one bit!

So try to imagine that every moment of your life is like the moment when your girlfriend said 'I love you!.'..continue to be in a cheerful mood always. The energy field that forms around your body would then act like an armour, protecting you from the harmful words of others.

This energy field is not a piece of fiction as some may wonder. The camera invented by the Russian expert named Kirlan has proved this point. Every person has an aura around him — either positive or negative. This has been revealed by Kirlan photography.

Reflections

Yoga of Wisdom
Learn to see the tricks of your Mind

Yoga of Action
Learn to feel Silence and you will hear the Divine answer .Two people cannot hate each other if there is silence.

SPRING OF ENERGY

How can you strengthen your energy field and maintain enthusiasm at an optimum level always?

Hindu scriptures mention: 'Drishti - Shrushti Vaada.' 'Drishti' means Vision. 'Shrushti' means Creation; 'Vaada' means dialogue.

What we see becomes the creation. We become whatever we envision ourselves to be. To make it more specific, whatever we imagine ourselves to be, we slowly move towards it.

Say to yourself, 'I am full of energy and good cheer!' Believe in what you say and you will surely remain full of energy. Does it seem to be impractical? Have a look at this example.

A young man who had a good sleep, woke up early in the morning and completed his daily exercise. He dressed and started for his work. His neighbour who accompanied him asked with great concern, 'You seem to be dull. Are you not keeping well?'

Next, he met his friend at the end the street, who asked him, 'What is wrong? Your face appears so tired!'

The young man entered the office and the receptionist also enquired, 'Are you suffering from fever? Your eyes are sunk. Why did you not take a day off from work?'

By now, the young man really began to feel sick. So he took a day off from office and returned home.

This is not a piece of fiction. It was an experiment conducted on him without his knowledge to observe the influence of mind over matter.

This is a true example of how our thoughts affect our body. At times, it works vice versa and our body affects our thoughts.

Let us take an example of the nail biting habit, while in tension. Once the habit becomes ingrained, even if one bites nails when normal, tension will somehow creep into one's mind. Some persons are in the habit of sitting down with their jaw resting on their hand whenever they feel dull. Even if they happen to sit casually like that, they would begin to feel dull for no reason at all. Why go that far? Don't we all feel like wearing fresh clothes while going out?

In a second it would be possible to spring energy from within.

You may all have witnessed 'fire-walking' during temple festivals. Those devotees who participate in fire walking may not be professionals. Yet, the moment they decide to 'fire-walk', they imbibe the enthusiasm of excellent performers. From where do they get this? From their minds of course!

Most of the ideas discussed here are already known to all of us. Still, we are unable to pull ourselves out of depression and feel very desolate. We simply drown in our sorrows. Why is this?

Most of us are particular that our point of view should win rather than being happy. Being happy is not our first priority.

A very rich man known to me owns a big house in a central locality in Bangalore. It is a family heritage. Even if he were to sell a small out-house adjacent to the large house, he would make at least half a million dollars. With that money, he could live royally. But his point of view is, that an ancestral inheritance should never be sold.........

So, what is his situation today? Though he lives in a big house, he struggles to pay even the property tax, telephone bill, electricity bill etc., as there is no income from his ancestral inheritance. A real pity!

There are some who go to the extreme end of committing suicide in order to prove their point of view.

We must consider that our happiness is more important than our beliefs. 'What is the problem as long as our happiness and contentment are obtained through just means?' Once we cultivate this attitude, there will be no dearth of energy and enthusiasm in our lives!

Reflections

Yoga of Wisdom
Allow enthusiasm to grow and prosper in your acre of diamonds.

Yoga of Action
Sing a song of enthusiasm and create magic around it.

SING, DANCE, LAUGH AND CRY!

(Q)uite some time back, I was in Hyderabad to talk on imagination and creativity. The number of participants was very small, which was unusual for my talks. When I sought the reason, I was told that people were interested in practical life issues. They were under the impression that imagination and creativity were more essential for those who are painters, poets, writers, film artists..... Ordinary people do not require them. So, not many had turned up for the talk.

How wrong this concept is! Take a toothpaste. The advertisers use so many techniques to popularise their brand 'This paste strengthens the gums', 'removes bad breath', 'kills germs', 'cleans up the yellow scales', 'provides fresh breath', 'mint-flavoured', 'more foamy', 'specially made for children......!'

Imagination is essential not only for those who are involved in trade and business, but for every one, including government employees, housewives, students, retired persons....

Recently I met a young girl in Madras during one of my 'LIFE Programs.' Her parents lived in a small town near Thanjavur. She was a skilled artist. She stayed with her aunt in Madras who ran an Arts & Crafts school. She was learning how to manage the school. Her aunt showered her with love and treated her as one of her own daughters. The problem came when the young girl happened to talk to men who visited the school, the aunt felt upset and scolded her.

'I am an educated girl. I know what is good and what is bad for me. When I converse with men who come here, it is purely professional and not with any ulterior motive. No man can cheat me. So please don't get worried...' the girl explained clearly to her aunt many times over, requesting her to avoid getting tense for nothing. Her words had no effect on her aunt, whatsoever!

'Now, what do I do? No matter how well I explain things, gently, with love and affection, or in anger and frustration, nothing seems to work. How do I make her understand the situation?' the girl asked.

Though she was capable of creating paintings and pictures with a lot of imagination, she found it impossible to make her aunt understand something, which she considered right and proper. Here, she had failed to use her imagination effectively.

I initiated a small role-play, with the girl as the aunt and myself as the girl. From that she drew many ideas as to how her aunt could be made to see her point of view, and be calmed.

The reason for my narration is, in our lives, we encounter many persons who prove to be irksome. The next door neighbour who insists on playing his music at full volume; the men across the street who regularly dump their garbage in front of our gates; the quarrelsome wife; nagging husband; disobedient kids. In order to handle all these, we cannot hope to succeed by employing one common method. If we consider them as challenges to our creative ability and ponder deeply, we may find hundreds of ways to handle the situations!

Recall the kindergarten story of the thirsty crow. It is all about creativity. The thirsty crow, tired after searching for water, finally finds a little water at the bottom of a tall jar. It then drops pebbles into the jar to raise the level of the water. If this is not creativity, what else can be?

There are certain basic necessities for the growth of creative thinking.

Our brain can be divided into four parts. While we think rationally, the logical part of the brain functions. While planning, the second part works. The third part of the brain has to do with intuition. This is related to what we call 'gut-feeling', 'a little bird told me.....' The fourth part of the brain functions while we are emotional...laughing, crying, dancing, singing....

Generally, men use the logic and planning side of the brain more often. So, for them the first two parts of the brain are more functional. Women are highly emotive. Thus, intuitive and emotive part of the brain, i.e., the third and fourth portions are more effective in women.

We need to utilize all the four parts equally in order to be fully effective. Many of us cannot accept that we can and should laugh out loud, cry freely, sing, dance, run, jump..... What would be the result of this approach? The fourth part of the brain would remain unused and thus become dysfunctional. This is not healthy. Only by using all the four parts, can we become complete human beings. Our brains would then function in their full capacities. This understanding is necessary for the full blossoming of one's creative imagination.

So, while you are reading a really good and humorous book, laugh loudly. If you feel sad, cry without restraint ... of course, in privacy. If you feel happy, sing aloud and dance around, if you wish! There is nothing to be ashamed about dancing. Lord Shiva who we worship is none other than Nataraja, the King of Dance! A dancing deity.

Reflections

Yoga of Wisdom
*Being creative is to respect
the creator in you.*

Yoga of Action
*Give yourself a break and start seeing
things differently.*

Contemplation

Better be with enlightened people in prison than fools in paradise.

Education means destroying the problematic mind and not stuffing the memory.

Imagination is more important than knowledge.
.. Albert Einstein.

Imagination, inspiration and commitment to excel is the mother of creativity.

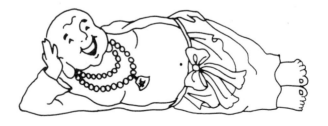

A WITCH
WITHIN OUR MIND!

Some of you may be familiar with the story of Rapunzel. She was a great beauty. When she was young, a witch took her away from her parents and put her in a tall tower, deep in a dense forest. The tower did not have doors or stairs. Right on top, there was just one single window. Rapunzel eventually grew into a beauty, with skin like fresh blown roses and long hair like spun gold.

Rapunzel grew up knowing nothing about the outside world. The witch used to visit her through a window, climbing by grasping her long hair. But the witch did not reveal to her as to how beautiful she was. She was very possessive of her and did not ever want her to leave the tower. She thought, if Rapunzel learnt of her true nature, or of the world outside she would escape from her and go away. There was nothing in the tower that could reflect anything; so the girl had never even seen her own face. All she knew was the witch.

The witch constantly told Rapunzel how ugly she was and demeaned her totally, from dawn to dusk. Rapunzel had no choice but to believe all this. She used to feel sad that God had created her ugly and cried bitterly, all day long.

One fine day, a prince happened to come to the forest to hunt. Having lost his way, he chanced by the tall tower, where he glimpsed the fair face of Rapunzel and fell in love with her, at the very first sight. He climbed to the top of the tower, just the same way that the witch used to, using the girl's long hair. He told her how beautiful she was and that he loved her dearly.

For the first time in her life, Rapunzel realized how good-looking she was. Thereafter, they met often and their love grew deep and strong. The story ends, after many mishaps, with the prince releasing Rapunzel from the prison and marrying her. And as in all fairy tales, they lived happily ever after!

Now, you may wonder why I had to relate this fairy tale here! Before we go into the reason for the story, let us remind ourselves of the ideas on creativity that we shared earlier.

A boy was studying in primary school. For some reason, he was unable to score good marks in English language. His family members as well the teachers at school told him repeatedly that he was no good in English. This was done again and again till he completed his college.

Now, is there any difference between this and what the witch used to tell Rapunzel? This is known as 'Negative Belief.'

There is a witch in us- 'Negative Belief.' There is a prince in us; 'Creativity.' Our mind, if it becomes repetitive, can be a prison in which the beautiful Rapunzel would be trapped.

This young boy, just like Rapunzel, believed what others said about him as the whole truth and nothing but the truth. He even avoided reading English newspapers and magazines. He refused to speak even a few words in English, to others. If at all, he faced a situation where he was forced to speak in English, he would slip away, excusing himself saying, 'I cannot speak in English.'

This way of frequently telling oneself is known as 'Repetitive Thinking.' The tower represents repetitive thinking.

It is like oxen bound to a wooden log in an oil-mill, moving in the same track again and again. Just as Rapunzel was imprisoned in a tall tower, this young man was imprisoned by his own repetitive thinking. Due to this thinking, he never even attempted to learn English.

To develop this boy's self confidence, a prince must come along. That prince is what I call 'Creativity.' Only this prince can overcome the witch that is 'Negative Belief.' The prince - `Creativity' alone can release the princess -`Ability' from the prison of `Repetitive Thinking.'

Feeling shy to speak in English is only one such example! Life is replete with many examples. When we are faced with people such as a prejudiced boss, a debtor who refuses to repay the loan, a spouse who is always rude....., if we think with a repetitive mind that one can never change such characters...we cannot find any solution to our problems. In order to plan how to approach them, think clearly; the most essential tool for all of us is 'creativity.'

Well, what is it that blocks creativity in us?

One main enemy that blocks imaginative thinking is a
'Repetitive Mind.' This is what prevents us from viewing any
issue from a totally new perspective. The oxen-bound-at-
the-oil-mill is the block!

Reflections

Yoga of Wisdom
A repetitive mind is a psychological prison.

Yoga of Action
Creatively dig into new ideas and create your own beautiful World.

Contemplation

Acting on a good idea is better than having a good idea.

.. Robert Half.

The most difficult things to open are a closed mind and heart.

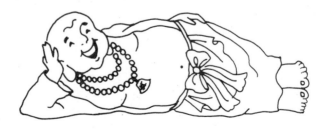

WHO GETS THE PIECE OF CAKE?

Ⓣhere are people who lie down and slumber all the time, saying that everything is so boring.

Particularly during college and school holidays, in every house one can hear these words 'It is so boring to sit at home! 'Well, what does it mean?' To put it simply, doing things that we do not relish...such as, sitting idle, lying in bed aimlessly, whiling away time.... make life boring.

When we do things that we enjoy, life is not boring. But many of us fail to understand this simple fact. Even if some jobs we enjoy doing, are available and awaiting our intervention, we keep postponing them.

'If there is something you enjoy doing, do not postpone it!' is a saying. There is a funny story to explain this simple fact.

An Englishman, an Arab and an Indian were together. They found a small piece of Cake, a rare delicacy in that region. It was too small to be shared amongst the three of them.

So, they came to a consensus; 'Right now, we shall put the piece of Cake in a container and go to sleep. And whoever gets the best dream can have the cake.' With this decision, they all went to sleep.

Next morning, they all met to share their dreams. First the Englishman began. 'Last night, God appeared in my dream. He took me to his garden and showed me lots of wonderful things', he said.

Next the Arab said, 'God appeared in my dream also. But I took Him to my garden and showed Him Arabian magics!'

Finally the Indian began to speak. He said, 'God appeared in my dream too! But we did not go to any garden. He only looked at me and said, 'You fool! With such a delicate piece of cake right in front of you, you are lying down and dreaming! First get rid of your sleep. Go at once and eat that Cake!' When God Himself ordered me, how could I disobey Him? So I got up silently and ate the Cake.

The other two were completely baffled. They hurriedly opened the container and the Cake was missing!

Let us take the message from this story.

Do not postpone being happy.

Whichever activity provides us with great joy, we should never postpone doing it.

One can slightly modify this sentence to read 'Whichever activity you do, do it with joy and total involvement.' Then the very word 'boredom' would simply disappear from your dictionary.

If you do not know swimming, then go and learn to swim. If you have never gone boating, then do that. Or learn to play some musical instrument. Try to learn a new language. If you find all this too cumbersome, then at least go and meet a friend you have not seen for years! This will help you overcome boredom.

A Zen monk was on his death-bed. All his disciples thronged around him, in sorrow. They asked, 'Master! What is your last sermon?'

The monk, instead of replying to their question, asked for a sweet. When the sweet was brought, he looked at it with elation, like a small child. He then ate it, bit by bit, fully savouring its taste, tapping his hands rhythmically. Thereafter, he simply died. Eating a sweet is a very ordinary affair. Even that should be done with total involvement and relish. This was the last message that the monk wished to convey.

It is not only those who sit idle at home that are bored. Doing the same thing over and again for years together can also be boring like oxen-bound-in-the-oil mill.

Every human being has four dimensions in his life - Intimate life, Family life, Professional life and Social life. A person has to live through all the four dimensions of life.

While maintaining a clean living room, bedroom and kitchen, if the toilet is left unattended, what would happen? The foul smell from it, would ruin the atmosphere of other rooms that are kept so well! Wouldn't it? Similarly, even if one of the four dimensions of life is unfulfilled and empty, it would make the whole life distasteful and meaningless.

Treat life holistically. Learn to create a balance in all aspects of life. Don't get lost in one aspect of life and neglect the other; for one will start affecting the other.

Reflections

Yoga of Wisdom
Learn to enjoy little things; there are many of them.

Yoga of Action
*Enjoy yourself and enjoy today. Do not waste time
by grieving over a bad yesterday.
Who knows, tomorrow may not be as good as today.*

OH, GOD!

We pray to God. But most often, what is the quality of our prayers?

'Oh God! My wife is not good. Change her character. My children are not okay. Change their behaviour! The next-door neighbour is a brute. He is always fighting with me for nothing, please change him...'

We continuously keep nagging God to change others around us. To put it in another way, we are actually saying, 'God, you are keeping quiet by simply looking at all these! Please change yourself! Change yourself from being idle and do something favourable to me!'

Can you see how strange all this is?

Do we pray to change ourselves or to change God?

Knowing well that prayer is not meant to change God, we even persist with our foolishness.

There are others who declare proudly to every one they meet, 'I offer prayers for an hour every day without fail .. come rain or shine.' For them, even adorning the sacred ash is a matter of image. Hence they are married to the rituals of prayer, rather than imbibing the spirit of prayer.

There is yet another kind of prayer.

A lady was sitting by the side of a window watching the scene outside. The mountain was very pretty. Suddenly she remembered a proverb 'Prayers can move mountains.' She wanted to test God.

Closing her eyes, she knelt on the floor and prayed thus: 'God, if you move this mountain that is between the sea and my house, I would get the sea breeze. So please move the mountain!'

When she opened her eyes, the mountain was intact, without moving an inch. She smiled and said, 'I was very sure that the mountain would not move. The saying that prayers can move mountains is all baloney. My hunch that it would not, was correct!' and patted herself.

She prayed with a conviction that prayer would not move the mountain. The essence of the prayer came from disbelief rather than belief. Here, prayer was a mere ritual and not an expression of commitment.

Again, there is another kind of prayer. A Prayer just for prayer's sake – a sheer mechanical one. That is to pray with minds wandering all over, with holy chants being only on the lips ….

A disciple performed great service to humanity. The Head of the Church wished to give him a gift and presented him with a miraculous horse.

That horse was very pious.

When one said, 'Oh God!' the horse would run very fast. If one wanted the horse to run continuously, one had to say, 'Oh God, Oh God' repeatedly. Similarly, if one wanted to stop the horse, it was not enough to pull the reins back. The horse would only stop if one said, 'Thank you, God.'

The head of the church explained the language the horse understood and left. The disciple wished to ride the newly acquired horse and mounted it and said, 'Oh God.' The horse galloped. The disciple felt as though he was flying in air. Highly excited, he repeatedly said, 'Oh God, Oh God.' The horse galloped as fast as wind on the mountainous terrain. The disciple, who was earlier so enchanted with the ride, was shocked. The horse was racing towards a steep cliff. He tried in vain to hold back the reins to stop it. But the horse ran non-stop. Suddenly he recalled the words of the head of the church. Closing his eyes, he screamed, 'Thank you, God.' His voice echoed over the entire mountain range and the horse stopped at once. The disciple slowly opened his eyes and looked. He was at the edge of the cliff. The disciple froze in terror, and thinking how he escaped a great danger, he panted in relief saying, 'Oh God.' The next instant, the conditioned horse plunged headlong into the gorge.

This story only goes on to show how mechanically we use the name of God, and how we pray without fully knowing the meaning of it.

How do we pray? To this question, the reply can be found in the life of Kabir. Kabir says:

'There was not a place left where I did not seek God. Temples, tanks, towers, all over the place I roamed around looking for God. I could not find Him.' Finally exhausted, I said to myself, 'So what if I cannot find God? Let me decide myself that I am a God realised person and experience Him.' I began to live as loving, as silent and as blissful as God. Godliness came into me of its own accord.

Lo, the miracle happened. Suddenly I heard God calling me 'Oh! Kabir, Oh, Kabir, where are you? I am searching for you.'

Kabir said, 'All along I was searching for you, Oh God; but now you are after me. I have realised the God within me and hence, I would have no more business with you.'

Modern psychology calls this as 'Act-As-If Theory.' The very centre of this theory is 'trust.' Trust you are blissful, silent and loving. This trust creates divine magic.

Do everything with trust. If you do not find what you are seeking, behave as though you have already found it. After that, you will surely find it! This is how the mystery of prayer works.

Reflections

Yoga of Wisdom
Mystery of prayer is magical.
Just trust it.

Yoga of Action
Trust is the essence to
understand mystery.

Contemplation

Do not postpone being happy.

Our prayers are so often mechanical.

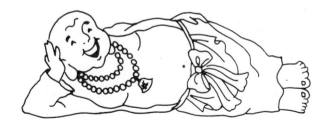

A BOOSTER OF ENTHUSIASM!

Swamiji! All around me there are howling packs of jackals. Business associates, family members and friends...one after the other; each of them has always betrayed me. When I think of all the loss, misery and shame suffered by me, my heart aches! I am unable to decide what is on top of my shoulders ... whether it is my head or a heavy boulder...my brain is fraught with worries. How do I escape this?

All that I can say is this:

By worrying, if your problems are resolved, please go ahead and worry. Do you know what happens when you worry all the time? Worry is like a small stone that turns into a huge granite boulder. All through the time that you worry, your failures, insults, pains and sorrows parade in front of your eyes, one after the other. Worry is like a rocking chair; keeps you busy, but takes you nowhere.

Whereas, if you are happy, the fruits of your labour, your success stories, happy moments, great achievements... play on your mental screen, one after the other!

Now tell me! When does your optimum capacity show up?...... When you are worried or when you are happy?

Only when you are happy, right?

All right! How to be happy? The first recipe for happiness is laughter. One should laugh heartily, laugh until muscles strain!

You might have heard of the 'Laughing Buddha.' There were three Buddhist monks. Just as Buddha got enlightenment under the Bodhi tree, these three monks got enlightenment through laughter. They later taught the world that laughing could be a way of meditation. They called it laughing meditation. They spread the message of laughter throughout their lives, far and wide.

One of the monks passed away. The other two sat on either side of his body and began to laugh. The town people were angered by this seemingly inappropriate behaviour and started abusing them. To which, the monks replied:

'Our friend spent his whole life in helping people to understand the message of laughter. We are laughing because

- he has won the game of death first
- the message from his life was laughter
- if we do not bid him farewell with laughter his soul will laugh at us that we are trapped like others by seriousness.

Thus, we are laughing, as per his wish before his death.'

It was time to conduct the final rites for the funeral. The monk had said before his death, 'Since I was laughing throughout my life, laughter has cleansed all impurities from within me. So please do not wash my body with water.'

Accordingly, his body was not bathed, but taken directly to the funeral pyre. As the body was lit by fire, suddenly there was a burst of crackers from the pyre. Yes! The monk had fastened crackers to his body under his flowing robes before his death. He had done so to make every one laugh even after his death! Hence he was called the 'Laughing Buddha.'

Apply any amount of cosmetics if you wish to.... face powder, eye shadow, and lipstick to enhance your beauty...but would they all become equal to one genuine smile? There is no better cosmetic than a genuine smile!

Just acquainted persons, if they meet and laugh at some jokes... chances are that they would become good friends!

Not only does laughter fetch you new friends, but it also strengthens old friendships.

'Laugh aloud and your disease will disappear' is a Tamil proverb. Today, hospitals in USA are beginning to realize the truth of this proverb! In some hospitals, Humour Nurses are appointed. Their job is to make the patients laugh!

Whenever feelings of anger, sadness or lethargy strike, try reading a good joke and laugh heartily! Do not complain that the joke is not good enough to invoke a hearty laugh. Simply use a joke as an excuse and laugh. When one laughs, certain chemical changes take place in the body. These changes dissolve all negative feelings such as anger, sorrow and depression. You would feel totally refreshed, like as if you had just bathed in a waterfall cascading from the top of a mountain: and the body would be rejuvenated!

Reflections

Yoga of Wisdom
*Life lived happily is the measure
of a successful life.*

Yoga of Action
*Discover the treasure of happiness within.
Happiness is the result of not investing in misery.*

THE DANCE OF NATARAJA!

ℳany people smoke. Some drink alcohol.

If you ask them why they smoke or drink, they would reply that they smoke because they feel bored, or because they wish to forget their worries or to just feel relaxed. Whenever their body or mind feels depressed or dull, or when they feel stressed, they wish to change that state. In order to do that, the only way they know is smoking or drinking.

When the mental rhythm or bodily rhythm remains static for a prolonged period of time i.e., in the same wavelength, it would be boring. Then lethargy is certain to set in. Sometimes, a meaningless sense of depression also may engulf a person. This kind of situation does not make any one happy. So they think if there could be some change in the mental rhythm or bodily rhythm, that would create some joy, some enthusiasm. And for that, they surrender themselves to cigarettes and liquor.

There is no doubt that cigarettes and liquor create certain changes in the body rhythm. But, at the same time, they also lead to some bad side effects. Don't they?

Is there anything that could change the body rhythm and infuse enthusiasm without any bad side effects?

Yes, there is! Surely there is!

One such important activity is dance.

Now, don't frown, saying, 'What?.... dance?'

Don't turn away saying that dance is something not appropriate to our culture. In fact, our culture and dance are interwoven so deeply! Bharata Natyam, Kuchipudi, Odissi, Mohini Aattam, Yakshagana ..., are a few of the multifarious dance forms that took roots and flourished in our country.

The word 'Hindu' has many meanings. One of the important meanings is 'It is that which destroys something which keeps us low.'

What is it that takes away our enthusiasm, excitement, energy and self-confidence and thereby keeps us low?

Laziness, self-pity, depression and other similar feelings. Don't you agree? First, we must destroy these negative feelings.

Just look at the form of Lord Nataraja. The Idol of Lord Nataraja signifies:

The demon under the feet of the dancing Nataraja means the demon is the power that takes away the energy from us!

The dancing Lord holds a flame in one of his four hands - it represents the fire of understanding. The saffron coloured robes worn by the Saints (who have renounced the world) also depict the same – the fire – the fire of knowledge.

The Damaru, drum held in another hand by Nataraja - signifies waves of ecstasy-an expression of enlightenment.

The third hand of Nataraja showing Abhaya Mudra declaring - 'Live Life Fearlessly.'

The fourth hand of Nataraja points towards the feet of the Lord - represents the quality of surrendering. To live fearlessly is possible if one knows the value of surrender.

What and where to surrender?

Ego. Surrender ego at the feet of the lord.

If we destroy the demon who pulls us down, we get into a gambolling enthusiasm. This enthusiasm leads to happiness.

At this juncture, I am reminded of a nursery rhyme taught to tiny tots. The rhyme goes like this:

What time is it?

It is the time to be 'happy'

The time to be happy is 'now'

The place to be happy is 'here'

The way to be happy is to 'make some one happy and create a heaven right here'.

There is a particular type of dance known as 'Sufi Dance.' The steps and movements of this dance are choreographed to simulate motions that seem to discard all the problems that we have. The end of the dance symbolises giving the joy flowing out of our hearts to every one, like Santa Claus does.

Now you may well ask me, 'Swamiji! You say that dancing would change the body rhythm which would make enthusiasm spring forth...in that case, what is the difference between dances performed in discotheques and the dance of Nataraja?'

In a disco when you dance, your sex centre is activated and you dance for fun. In a meditative dance, your bliss centre is activated. Dance becomes an expression of joy.

But if we dance like Lord Nataraja, with the mastery of our lower mind - the demon, then the dancer disappears, and only dance remains. Such a dance is a dance born out of ecstasy, a forgotten language.

Well, how do we dance like that?

If you dance for happiness, you would not get happiness. So at the outset, dance with happiness. That is to say, do not dance for happiness! Dance out of happiness!

Reflections

Yoga of Wisdom
Understand bliss by treating each day like as if it were the first day of your honeymoon and the last day of your vacation.

Yoga of Action
Keep your mind empty and let joy find you.

Contemplation

The worst boss anyone can have is a bad habit.

Habits are either the best of servants or the worst of masters. Develop a habit to be happy & pure.

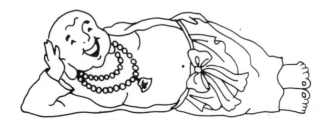

WHAT ARE YOU – SIEVE OR WINNOW?

A disciple asked his Master –

What is the power that makes the eyes see?

'The eye of the eye!'

What is the power that makes the ears hear?

'The ear of the ear!'

The Master then asked the disciple – 'Did you understand what I said?'

'No, I did not!' said the disciple in confusion.

'If you did not understand my explanation, it means you have understood.

If you have understood, it means you have not understood!'

Do you think that the above dialogue is between people under the influence of narcotics?

Well, the above dialogue is found in Kena Upanishad, one of the Hindu Scriptures!

Human beings possess one special faculty that none of the other living beings have. That is the ability to think. A computer on the ground controls the satellite thousands of kilometres away. It can carry out all the instructions set by humans, perfectly like a slave. But it cannot think. The only living beings on earth that are capable of thinking are human beings!

How many of us utilise this thinking capacity?

In order to make a disciple think, the Rishis devised many methods. Many such strategies are found in Kena Upanishad. Once the thinking door is closed, we become fools. Almost like the servant in the following anecdote!

There was a trader who sold rabbits. One day, he gave a rabbit to his servant and said, 'Go and deliver the rabbit to a lady and bring the cash in return, without fail. Here is the address.'

The servant, while going through a crowded market place, happened to collide with a man coming in the opposite direction. He fell down and the rabbit escaped from his hand.

The servant merely stood, watching the rabbit running away. The onlookers said, 'Hey, you idiot! Run and catch the rabbit!'

But the servant said unperturbed, 'So what, if the rabbit ran away? Where will the rabbit go? I still have the address given by my boss safe with me!'

Do you know why I have narrated this story?

So far, I have narrated several parables only to instil the moral values of the stories, in you. But, if you take only the story and keep aside the morals, you would be like the servant who was satisfied in keeping the address intact and allowing the rabbit to escape – you too would have felt content reading the stories but would not have imbibed the essential moral from them.

Ignorance is a very serious curse. Being foolish is a greater punishment. The strange thing is, we are solely responsible for inflicting on ourselves, the curse as well as the punishment.

Ramesh was a clerk in a private firm. One day, he was not well. His colleagues suggested to him, 'It is already 3 O'clock. Today is Saturday and the manager would not return. So why don't you simply go home?'

With a lot of hesitation and fear, Ramesh left the office. As he reached his house, he saw the manager's car parked, outside. 'I could be in for trouble!' he thought, as he went stealthily behind his house. Slowly he moved a curtain aside and peeped through the window. He witnessed the ghastly sight of the manager in bed, with his wife.

He ran to the office and told his colleagues, 'God! Am I lucky! I was almost caught by the manager! Luckily, I escaped in time, before he noticed me!'

Now, who caught whom?

When one is foolish, look what price one has to pay for that!

In this world, it is not enough just to own degrees awarded by the university. One should also be intelligent.

So, read a lot! Think deeply. Work with purpose! All the twelve months of the year in your life would be like springtime!

The Guru told his disciple who was graduating from the Gurukula – (The masters place where a student spends many years studying) after many years of study:

'Be like a Winnow (grain-sorting pan) and not like a Sieve!'

Do you know the meaning of this?

A Sieve allows all the good stuff to pass through its pores while retaining the waste materials within. A Winnow (grain-sorting pan) on the other hand, discards the stones, chaff...., and retains only good grain.

What are you? Sieve or Winnow?

Reflections

Yoga of Wisdom
Knowledge is the ability to distinguish between the essential and unessential. Ignorance stiffens thinking and makes you lose the flexibility to see the essential and the unessential clearly.

Yoga of Action
Focus and act from what is essential. Then the mind will be wisely employed. Oh, Mind Relax Please!

Contemplation

We get a word, lose its meaning and thereby miss the context.

An unwise person empties his head every time he opens his mouth.

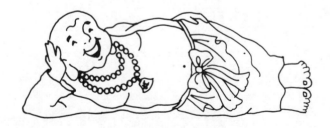

A view of Nirguna Mandir at Bangalore

300/18, 6th Main, 14th Cross
Vyalikaval, Bangalore – 560 003
Phone: 91-80-2344 4112.
E-Mail: prasannatrust@vsnl.com
www.swamisukhabodhananda.org

Prasanna Trust is a registered social charitable trust set up with the objective to re-look at various facets of Indian philosophy and culture for effective transformation of individuals in particular and the society in general.

We have made our presence primarily through :

- Transformative Education

- Social Oriented Service

TRANSFORMATIVE EDUCATION

a) LOOKING AT LIFE DIFFERENTLY

It is a 2 days workshop on personal effectiveness through interactions and meditations. An experience oriented, non-religious program designed to enhance productivity, handling stress, personal well-being and organisational synergy. It focuses on bringing forth the outer winner leading to creativity and an inner winner to meditative consciousness.

b) EXISTENTIAL LABORATORY

It is a 4-days residential retreat set amidst natural surroundings to experience oneself through a series of dynamic and passive meditations in order to see connectivity with nature, to heal and release the inner child, to realise innocence and wonderment in all walks of life based on the Upanishad truths - Chakshumathi Vidya.

c) CORPORATE HARMONY AND CREATIVITY

It is a 2 days comprehensive workshop for senior level executives to harness creativity and harmony in today's competitive work environment and preparing them for globalisation.

d) YOUTH PROGRAMME

It is a 3 days program based on multiple intelligence. The program develops the hidden talent and skill in a child; to enable the child to face the world with confidence as each child is unique.

e) OH, MIND RELAX PLEASE!

It is a 1 day seminar based on unique techniques to transform from ordinary to extra-ordinary, dealing with fear and conflicts and converting them as challenges..

f) RELATIONSHIP SEMINAR

An exclusive workshop for couples, so as to discover intimacy and togetherness in a relationship.

g) TEACHERS' TRAINING PROGRAMME

A 5 days workshop designed to train and develop an individual as Pracharak or teacher for spreading the universal message for the benefit of society.

h) MANTRA YOGA PROGRAMME – A Holistic approach to Life

A workshop based on five powerful Mantras to help in enhancing health, unlocking the blissful centre, increasing intuitive ability, creating wealth and divinity in oneself and others. This program is conducted in English and also in many Indian languages by well trained Pracharaks.

i) NIRGUNA MANDIR – A Meditation Centre for Learning
* Unfolding the traditional texts of the Bhagavad Gita & the Upanishads as is relevant in today's living context.
* Workshops to bring forth creativity and awareness among youth, women and parents through a spiritual paradigm.
* Research to foster universal love through an inter-religious forum.
* Orientation programs for trainers and social workers.
* Spiritual inputs to deal with phobia, fear, trauma, drug and alcoholic abuse.

SOCIAL ORIENTED SERVICE

a) CHILD CARE CENTRE - A HOME FOR HOMELESS - PRASANNA JYOTHI:
Nurturing lives of little angels who have been orphaned due to the paradox of circumstances. Uncared girls who otherwise would have withered away are growing into enthusiastic, intelligent, celebrative and responsible children.

b) VOCATIONAL TRAINING FOR CHILDREN:
In order to keep abreast with the fast changing face of the world, it is proposed to give the children of Prasanna Jyothi training in office automation & allied area of skills.

We seek support of individuals, business houses, institutions and invite them to be part of this noble vision of creating an atmosphere to impart our culture and thus contributing to the society we build.

*Contribution to **Prasanna Trust** account is exempted from Income Tax under Section 80 (G)*

TITLES OF SWAMIJI'S WORKS

BOOKS

Meditation *(from Bhagavad Gita) (also in Tamil & Telugu)*
Karma Yoga *(based on Bhagavad Gita)*
Wisdom through Silence
(Commentary on Dhakshina Murthy Stotram)
Oh, Life Relax Please!
(also in Hindi, Tamil, Telugu, Gujarati and Marati)
Oh, Mind Relax Please!
(also in Tamil, Telugu, Kannada, Malayalam, Hindi, Marati & Gujarati)
Looking Life Differently *(also in Tamil)*
Stress Management – A bullet proof Yogic Approach
Art of Wise Parenting
Agame Relax Please! *(in Tamil)*
Kutumbave Relax Please! *(in Kannada & Telugu)*

AUDIO
TRADITIONAL UNFOLDMENT

Gayatri Mantra *(also in regional languages)*
Maha Mruthyunjaya Mantra *(also in regional languages)*
Om Gam Ganapate Namaha *(also in regional languages)*
Om Krishnaya Namaha *(also in regional languages)*
Om Shivaya Namaha *(also in regional languages)*
Mantra Chants
Trataka Yogic Technique
Shiva Sutras
Essence of Bhagavad Gita
Guru Purnima

MEDITATION

Brahmayagna	Maha Visarjana Kriya
Navratri Upasana	Meditation, the Music of Silence
Bhakti Yoga	Vedic Vision to Pregnant women
Mantra Healing	Yoga Laya

OCCULT TEACHINGS

Seven Chakras of Hindu Psychology
Symbolism of Hindu Rituals
Essence of Hinduism
Who am I?
Healing Hurt through Gayatri Mantra
Handling insecurity through Mruthyunjaya Mantra
Handling crisis through Taraka Mantra

MANAGEMENT –
A NEW LOOK THROUGH SPIRITUAL PARADIGM

Self Confidence through Hypnosis
Stress Management
Art of Parenting
People Management – an enlightened approach
Creating a Happy Marriage
Hypnosis and Relationship
Living in Freedom – an Enquiry
LIFE series

VIDEO (in VCD form)

Suffering to Surrender
Jokes to Joy – Navarasa
Discouragement to Encouragement
Worry to Wisdom
Stress Management through Spirituality
Seeds of Wisdom
Looking Life Differntly
A Balanced Man
Vedanta – the dynamics of living
Inner Awakening
Harmony in Chaos

Swamiji's workshop empowers one to be
Effective, Creative & Celebrative in all walks of life.

'LIFE' - a two-days workshop on how to use the mind for Success and Satisfaction

Objective of the Seminar:

Outer Winner

◆ The art of powerful goal setting.

◆ Decision-making, Team building.

◆ Divine principles of worldly achievement.

◆ Interpersonal skills & Effective communication

◆ How to deal with difficult people.

◆ Possibility thinker.

Inner Winner

◆ The art of being blissful, restful and loving.

◆ The art of healing psychological wounds.

◆ Mind management

◆ Worry management.

◆ Fear management.

◆ Meditation to bring about healthy inner healing and enlightenment.

What others say about the programme:

"Here's one Guru who's in tune with modern times."
— India Today.

"The unusual Swami from Bangalore is the latest Guru on the Indian Management scene."
— Business India.

"He has come to be hailed as the 'Corporate Guru'. The Management Swami has attempted to infuse the Corporate World with the much needed dose of ethics and spirituality."
— The Hindu.

**True Freedom Lies
In the Art of Looking at Life Afresh**

Glide through work pressures without the 'Sting of Stress'.
Say Yes to Growth, Achievement, Progress
Say No to Stress, Fatigue, Pressure.

Oh, Mind Relax Please!
a one-day workshop

**on transformation from ordinary to
extra-ordinary, dealing with
fear & conflicts and converting
them as challenges**

The programme offers:

◆ Impactful models to imbibe powerful insights, to bring forth creativity and spontaneity and discover life nourishing patterns rather than life defeating ones.

◆ Practical workouts using sciences of Pranayamas and Mudras as an antidote to the Yuppie Flu.

◆ Techniques to debug and update your inner softwares and to gracefully align to change.

◆ Processes to synergize a healthy mind with a healthy body.

For more details on Swamiji's in-house & public workshops, contact:

PRASANNA TRUST

\# 300/18, 6th Main, 14th Cross, Vyalikaval,
Bangalore – 560 003, INDIA
Ph: (080) 2344 4112 • Fax: (080) 2331 4293
E-mail – prasannatrust@vsnl.com
prmadhav@vsnl.com
Visit us at www.swamisukhabodhananda.org

NIRGUNA MANDIR

\#1, Nirguna Mandir Layout,
Near I Block Park, Koramangala,
Bangalore – 560 047, INDIA
Ph: (080) 2553 8976 / 2552 6102

At USA

E-mail: shakila8@hotmail.com
aruna@knology.net
parvathykancherla@yahoo.com

- - - - ✂ - - - - - - - - - - - - ✂ - - - - - -

Please send me information on

☐ **Seminar on LIFE program**
☐ **Seminar on YLP**
☐ **Seminar on Corporate Harmony & Creativity at work**
☐ **Books, Audio Cassettes, CD's, VCD's**

Name .... Title............................

Company..

Address ....

....

City.......................... State..............................Pin....................

Telephone (Off) .... (Res)..................................

Fax ....Email..